THE CL

# Stages of Change and Addiction

CLINICIAN'S MANUAL

THE CLINICAL INNOVATORS SERIES

# Stages of Change and Addiction

CLINICIAN'S MANUAL

*Carlo DiClemente*

Hazelden
Center City, Minnesota 55012-0176
1-800-328-9000
1-651-213-4590 (Fax)
www.hazelden.org

©2004 by Carlo DiClemente
All rights reserved. Published 2004
Printed in the United States of America

This published work is protected by copyright law. Unless a statement on the page grants permission to duplicate or permission has been obtained from the publisher, duplicating all or part of this work by any means is an illegal act.

To request permission, write to Permissions Coordinator, Hazelden, P.O. Box 176, Center City, MN 55012-0176. To purchase additional copies of this publication, call 1-800-328-9000 or 1-651-213-4000.

ISBN: 1-59285-171-1

08 07 06 05 04    6 5 4 3 2 1

Cover design by David Spohn
Interior design and typesetting by Kinne Design

## Contents

Editor's Note ................................................................. vi

Acknowledgments ............................................................ vii

Introduction ................................................................. ix

Chapter 1: The Transtheoretical Model: What Is It? ........................... 1

Chapter 2: The Movement into Addiction ..................................... 15

Chapter 3: Making an Assessment ............................................ 29

Chapter 4: Practical Strategies for Helping People in Recovery ............. 45

Appendix A: Alcohol (and Illegal Drugs) Decisional Balance Scale ......... 71

Appendix B: Brief Situational Confidence Questionnaire (BSCQ) .......... 75

Appendix C: Alcohol Abstinence Self-Efficacy Scale (AASE) ............... 77

Appendix D: The University of Rhode Island
            Change Assessment Scale (URICA) .......................... 81

Appendix E: Exercises
    Exercise 1: Readiness Ruler, 87
    Exercise 2: Decisional Balance Worksheet, 89
    Exercise 3: Change Plan Worksheet, 91

Notes ....................................................................... 93

About the Author ........................................................... 97

# Editor's Note

Hazelden's Clinical Innovators Series was designed with innovation in mind. The series features hot topics by leading, cutting-edge experts in the field. Each topic in the series is composed of a video, a clinician's manual, and a posttest offering continuing education hours (CEHs).

The *video* should be viewed first. It allows the viewer to participate in a workshop led by an internationally recognized, highly trained speaker. This particular workshop was filmed in front of a live audience.

The *clinician's manual* should be read after viewing the video. The manual is authored by the workshop speaker and expands on the material found in the video. As a NADAAC-approved provider, Hazelden offers continuing education hours for successful completion of the *posttest* based on the material, when applicable.

The Clinical Innovators Series is Hazelden's new, innovative professional development tool that can be used by everyone from chemical dependency counselors to psychologists to health-care professionals to clergypersons. The series' practical and applicable material will provide you with innovative techniques for your clinical practice that can be used immediately.

➢

# Acknowledgments

It truly has taken a village to create the body of knowledge and research that is the foundation of the transtheoretical model and the basis of the *Stages of Change and Addiction* video and clinician's manual in Hazelden's Clinical Innovators Series. I have been extremely fortunate to have had wonderful collaborators and co-investigators on the research projects and clinical applications that helped in the creation of the model and helped me understand the process of change.

Particularly helpful has been the seminal work done by Jim Prochaska, Wayne Velicer, Joe Rossi, John Norcross, and a host of students and staff in Rhode Island and Houston, Texas; the clinical application of the model in the alcoholism treatment program at the Texas Research Institute of Mental Sciences, with Jack Gordon, Glen Razak, and a wonderful staff of counselors open to innovation; the groundbreaking alcoholism treatment trial, Project MATCH, with its talented and creative investigators; and the recent multiple projects being conducted at the University of Maryland and other locations with Alan Bellack, Maureen Black, Joe Carbonari, Lisa Dixon, Pat Dolan-Mullen, Robert Fiedler, Melanie Gold, Jan Groff, Steve Havas, Carl Soderstrom, Mary Velasquez, Sally Vernon, Chudley Werch, and a terrific group of co-investigators, staff, and graduate students. This work has been enriched by the efforts of clinicians, researchers, program directors, and public health and prevention specialists around the world who have applied and used the model in their work and have given us feedback on its potential and problems.

The research, clinical applications, and dissemination of the model have been supported by a number of federal, state, and

## Acknowledgments

private institutions over the years. This financial support has been crucial for the development and testing of the model and in its diffusion. I would like to particularly acknowledge the support of the National Cancer Institute; the National Institute on Alcohol Abuse and Alcoholism; the Center for Substance Abuse Treatment; the Center for Substance Abuse Prevention; the National Heart, Lung, and Blood Institute; the Centers for Disease Control and Prevention; the Robert Wood Johnson Foundation; the National Institute on Drug Abuse; and the Departments of Health and Mental Hygiene in Texas and Maryland. Hopefully I have not missed anyone.

I would also like to thank all the folks at Hazelden who made the *Stages of Change and Addiction* video and clinician's manual possible. Richard Solly had the vision and convinced me to do this project. Yvonne Pearson has translated my thoughts and words into a very useful manual. Alex Scott and her staff have organized and produced a wonderful video that, with any luck, will reach many counselors and substance abusers and help them to make effective, positive, and lasting changes in their practices and lives.

The support and forbearance of my family during all the years when writing and conferences have been part of our life has been invaluable. Thanks to all of my family—especially Lyn, Cara, and Anna.

## Introduction

The transtheoretical model (TTM), more generally recognized by the name stages of change (SOC), is a powerful paradigm for understanding how addictions and recovery occur. Research suggests that people walk a predictable path whenever they intentionally change their behavior. Still, their steps don't always look the same from the outside. They may be slow, halting, abrupt, leaping, or erratic. Nevertheless, the territory they move through and the sequence of tasks they need to accomplish along the way are the same.

SOC conceptualizes the pathway by dividing the territory into five distinct stages and looks at the tasks people must accomplish to move through each successive stage. It also identifies the internal and external processes (the attitudes, thoughts, and behaviors) that people participate in as they walk through each of the five stages. Thus, SOC allows professionals to target specific processes of change according to where people are on their paths. In other words, treatment can be tailored to the stage any given person is in. It helps the professional know how to do the right thing at the right time.

Because it describes a generic pathway of intentional human behavior change, one of the strengths of SOC is that it allows clinicians to draw from many different therapeutic models. They may use motivational interviewing, Twelve Step facilitation, cognitive-behavioral therapy, or a variety of other theories. This model also empowers clients. It offers an alternative approach to viewing clients as in denial, resistant, or uncooperative, and views them instead as in a phase of change, even if that phase is not yet considering change.

## What to Expect in the *Stages of Change and Addiction Clinician's Manual*

*Stages of Change and Addiction* briefly explains the transtheoretical, or stages of change, model and how it can be used to help clinicians improve their practices. The manual presents this information in a user-friendly format and is designed for professionals in a wide variety of settings who are committed to treating people with substance abuse problems.

- *Chapter 1: The Transtheoretical Model: What Is It?* describes how people change—the stages they go through and the factors, both internal and external, which prompt change.

- *Chapter 2: The Movement into Addiction* focuses specifically on how people move through the stages of change while developing an addiction.

- *Chapter 3: Making an Assessment* looks at the characteristics of people in recovery and provides tips on how to accurately assess the stage of change a person is in.

- *Chapter 4: Practical Strategies for Helping People in Recovery* discusses how people move through the stages of change while recovering from an addiction. It also provides tools on matching interventions to their current stage of change.

- *Appendixes A, B, C, and D* include assessment tools to be used with clients to determine level of use and other key factors. *Appendix E* includes exercises that actively engage clients in exploring their substance use.

- *Notes* summarize source material for each chapter and each appendix.

A video, *Carlo DiClemente on Stages of Change and Addiction*, accompanies this clinician's manual. It's recommended that you view the video first and then read this clinician's manual. The video is designed to help you gain a wider understanding of the stages of change and how they relate to addiction, while this clinician's manual includes a more detailed explanation of stages of change and practical applications for your clinical practice.

➢

# 1

# The Transtheoretical Model: What Is It?

The transtheoretical model (TTM) is a description of how people change—the stages they go through and the factors, both internal and external, which prompt change. The model also describes the interaction between the factors. You might call it the grammar of change; it describes the "rules" people follow as they make changes.

TTM is based on research done by James Prochaska and me (the author) in the early 1980s. The research first attempted to identify the common elements of change in various theories, hence "transtheoretical." This soon turned into a broader exploration of intentional behavior change, especially of how people change addictive behaviors. We observed how nicotine-addicted smokers were able to quit smoking; we discovered that there were different stages everyone went through, whether they sought treatment or did it on their own. We also looked at data on people who stopped other addictions or harmful health-related behaviors and realized that these people went through the same stages of change.

It became evident that the change process could be divided into five distinct stages. This is true of people who quit smoking, who stop using alcohol or other drugs, who change their eating patterns, who integrate exercise into their lives, or who undergo any kind of change. This progression is especially useful in understanding addiction because people move through a similar set of stages when they become addicted, and when they successfully overcome an addiction.

## Four Dimensions of the TTM Model

The TTM model looks closely at the many circumstances and attitudes that interact with each other and influence how people move through the stages. It identifies what are called dimensions of change:

- The *stages of change* that people move through when they are making a change
- The *processes of change* that people experience, which enable them to change
- The *markers of change* that help identify where people are in the process
- The *context of change* (a person's internal life and external environment) that affects movement through each stage

Let's take a closer look at each of these dimensions.

### *Stages of Change*

The transtheoretical model is frequently called the stages of change model (SOC). The stages are sequential, and people move through them whenever they make any kind of behavioral change. This does not mean that people always march through them in a linear fashion. They may move back and forth between them or re-cycle through them. But they do move through all five of them before they have truly accomplished a change in behavior. The following paragraphs discuss these five stages.

*Precontemplation*
This first stage of change is really the precursor to change. People in precontemplation are not thinking about changing. They may not think they have a problem at all, or they may be only slightly aware that they have a problem. They may not be convinced there is any reason to change, they may feel discouraged about the possibility of changing, or they may simply not want to change. As far as they're concerned, their lives are working fine. For example, a man in the precontemplation stage may be unable or unwilling to see that his frequent drinking is affecting his performance at work or causing trouble in his marriage. A woman in the precontemplation stage may not recognize that her use of tranquilizers is keeping her from attending classes regularly. An adolescent may think anyone who suggests that his marijuana use is hurting his grades is crazy. In order to move to the next stage, these people must begin to see that there is a problem, get concerned about it, and then imagine that change is possible.

*Contemplation*
It's hard to see that change has begun in the contemplation stage. It's mostly internal. In this stage, people have become aware that they have a problem and they are thinking about whether or not they want to change. It's a stage marked by ambivalence. They're still drinking alcohol, using other drugs, or engaging in an addictive or negative behavior and they're not sure changing is worth the trouble. In this stage, they weigh the pros and cons. It is in part a rational process, but it is also an emotional process. It's a time when a person may gather a lot of information about treatment programs, but not actually enroll. A person may read books about the dangers of drug use, but keep on using anyway. A person may think about how miserable all that extra weight feels, read reviews of diet plans, and think, "Maybe one of these days."

Some may move through contemplation quickly, but others can spend a long time in this stage, even years. To move on to the next stage, a person must weigh the pros and cons and make a decision to change—an authentic decision that is based on the individual's own values and beliefs.

*Preparation*

In the preparation stage, change may still not be apparent to the observer, but it is to the person preparing to make the change. People are on the brink of making a real commitment in this stage. They have weighed the pros and cons and have decided that the negative aspects of the behavior outweigh the positive. It's a time of active planning; in this stage people decide what steps they will take in order to make the change. They may be making choices about whether they need treatment and which treatment they want to use. They may be abstaining from their substance use or experimenting with ways to cut back. This stage requires time, attention, energy, and commitment to follow through on a plan. The task people must accomplish in this stage is to summon the courage to follow through and create a viable plan for change.

*Action*

The action stage is where you see obvious behavior changes. People make drastic lifestyle changes. They throw away their cigarettes, pour the last bottle of vodka down the drain, quit buying chocolate, put on their running shoes in the morning, start going to Alcoholics Anonymous (AA), or enter a treatment program. The action stage is when people actually create new patterns of behavior, and creating a pattern only occurs over time. It requires repetition to establish a habit. This stage is generally seen as lasting about three to six months. The task of the action stage is to do something, then change the plan if necessary, and keep on going even when it's hard. The ultimate goal of this stage is to establish a pattern of new behavior.

*Maintenance*
During the maintenance stage, people consolidate the changes they have made. They are vigilant about situations or events that might trigger their desire to use. They remain careful to stay away from the bar they used to frequent if it stirs cravings. The new behaviors are practiced with such consistency that they become a natural, normal part of the person's life. This stage may last from six months to a lifetime, depending on the person and the behavior that is being changed. The maintenance stage isn't over until the behavior is the status quo, until the person is on autopilot. The task for this stage is to integrate the change into the total life context.

> **Precontemplation:** Not seeing a problem or need for change
> **Contemplation:** Seeing some benefits of change and considering whether to act
> **Preparation:** Making concrete plans to act soon
> **Action:** Doing something to change
> **Maintenance:** Working to maintain the change[1]

## *Processes of Change*
The processes of change are the experiences and activities that allow people to move through the stages of change. Processes of change fall into two groups. The first group is called *cognitive/experiential processes* and refers to a person's internal ways of thinking and feeling. These internal change processes are engaged primarily in the early stages. The second group is called *behavioral processes* and refers to what a person does—the observable, external actions. These occur more in the later stages of change. Still, both internal and external changes may occur in any of the stages.

| Cognitive/Experiential Processes | Behavioral Processes |
|---|---|
|  |  |
| Refers to a person's internal ways of thinking and feeling. | Refers to what a person does— the observable, external actions. |

Each group contains five specific processes. The labels are not always self-explanatory, so we will look at what each of them means.

*Cognitive/Experiential Processes (Internal)*

1. *Consciousness raising.* People gain awareness about themselves, a current behavior, a new behavior, or the need to change their behavior.
2. *Emotional arousal.* People experience strong emotional reactions to something about their current or new behavior. It can contribute to raising consciousness and to reevaluation of self and environment.
3. *Self-reevaluation.* People compare their behavior with their values and goals to see if they are in conflict. This is both a cognitive and an emotional process.
4. *Environmental reevaluation.* People notice the effects, both positive and negative, that their behaviors have on the people around them and on their environment. They are often motivated to change when they recognize that their behavior is important or hurtful to others.
5. *Social liberation.* This process refers to recognizing and accepting societal norms that encourage behavior change. In other words, how much does the person buy into society's notions about a particular behavior being acceptable or unacceptable?

*Behavioral Processes (External)*
1. *Stimulus control.* People alter or avoid situations or cues that are likely to trigger the behavior they want to change.
2. *Counterconditioning.* People change their response to a trigger. To do this, they may substitute healthy for unhealthy behaviors, such as using deep breathing when they feel very stressed instead of using a substance.
3. *Reinforcement management.* This refers to rewarding positive behavior changes. These can be literal rewards, such as asking for a medallion at an AA meeting or the good feeling experienced as a result of a positive behavior change.
4. *Self-liberation.* This process refers to making a choice and then taking responsibility to make a behavior change.
5. *Helping relationships.* People seek and develop relationships that support the changes they want to make.

It is important to note that prevention or treatment techniques are not the same as processes of change. A helping professional may use a technique to engage someone in the processes of change, and there may be hundreds of techniques for each process. But the processes themselves—from consciousness raising to counterconditioning—occur within the person or are undertaken by the person. The change processes are entirely the responsibility of the person. Thus, a technique may be both powerful and unsuccessful because people may respond differently to the same technique. For instance, you may use the technique of giving objective feedback to two people in the contemplation stage, and it may engage the process of self-reevaluation for one and not for the other who may rationalize it away. Still, to maximize the effectiveness of a technique, it is important to understand a client's stage of change and the processes of change that she must engage in to move through that stage and then to understand which technique fits that process.

Because the constructs identified by TTM are common to many different theories, the techniques used to engage these processes may also be drawn from many different theories. These include cognitive-behavioral therapy, motivational interviewing, Twelve Step facilitation, reality therapy, interpersonal therapy, and many others.

## Markers of Change

The third dimension of the TTM model is markers of change. They are particularly useful in assessing someone's stage of change, but they can also help in treatment planning. TTM identifies two markers of change: decisional balance and self-efficacy/temptation. You can observe the markers of change and how they alter as people move through the stages.

### Decisional Balance

This marker simply refers to the relative weight being given to the pros and cons in a risk-reward analysis. Is the person's overall position tilted more toward change or toward the status quo? On one hand, it seems like a good idea to make changes; on the other hand, it seems too difficult. As people move through the stages, this marker changes. In the precontemplation stage, for instance, the decisional balance is firmly in favor of the status quo. In the contemplation stage, a person tends to view the pros and cons as being equal. By the preparation stage, the pros for change are winning out, and the decisional balance is tipping toward a commitment to change. For instance, a woman in the contemplation stage may see her occasional weekends of bingeing on alcohol as a problem. She may list the frustration her husband feels with her and missing her kids' activities as pros for change, while listing the fun and the camaraderie with her friends as cons. When she moves into the preparation stage, she may add another pro for change, perhaps how awful she feels on the Mondays after the binges, which tips the decisional balance toward change. Or maybe she doesn't add any more pros, but she becomes more acutely aware of how the drinking is damaging her relationship with her husband and children, and the pros for change take on a heavier weight.

*Self-Efficacy / Temptation*
Self-efficacy refers to a person's confidence that he can perform a given behavior.[2] The question he puts to himself here is "Can I do it?" The answer may be yes, no, probably, maybe, or other shades of confidence in between. Confidence is dependent on the level of perceived difficulty to perform the behavior. This can vary from situation to situation. The level of self-efficacy gives important information about whether a person is going to move to another stage of change. While it's important information at any stage, research has shown that it is more important as a predictor in the later stages: preparation, action, and maintenance. In the precontemplation stage, a person has very low self-efficacy and temptation is typically high. By the time a person is in the maintenance stage, self-efficacy is much stronger and temptation is, for the most part, lower.

Temptation represents the strength of the desire or inclination to smoke, drink alcohol, use other drugs, or engage in another behavior in various situations. The question here is "How badly do I want to smoke, drink alcohol, or use other drugs when I see others doing it, when I am depressed, and so on?" Temptation generally decreases as self-efficacy increases, but not always. Understanding the level of temptation can help in forming plans during the preparation stage, as well as in predicting successful action and maintenance of behavior change.

## Context of Change

The fourth dimension of TTM, context of change, takes into account how the entire life of a person plays a role in the change process. It provides a wholistic look at change behavior. In other words, it allows you to see connections between other problem areas in a person's life and the specific behavior she is trying to change. It's important, however, not to get overwhelmed in trying to address multiple problems simultaneously with equal emphasis. You can be aware of the context, address additional problems to the extent necessary to help with the behavior the person wishes to target, but remain focused on the primary change that she wishes to make.

TTM looks at context in five areas of functioning[3]:

1. Current life situation
2. Beliefs and attitudes
3. Interpersonal relationships
4. Social systems
5. Enduring personal characteristics

### Current Life Situation

Problems and events in a current living situation affect the ability to move into a new stage. This area includes the emotional and mental status of a person. Here you take into account both strengths and weaknesses, such as financial and educational resources, intellectual ability, coping skills, and level of anxiety or depression. The greater the resources, the more support a person gets for change, and the fewer the problems and barriers he will face, increasing the chance of successful movement through the stages of change. So if a person has a high level of anxiety and has been using marijuana to calm himself, it makes quitting marijuana more difficult. On the other hand, change is supported if he is learning how to cope with his anxiety in therapy, taking a class in meditation, or getting acupuncture.

*Beliefs and Attitudes*
Assessing a person's belief system and basic values (i.e., beliefs about how change should happen, self, religion, God, and family) can help in understanding why a given person moves or does not move through various stages of change. Since values and beliefs influence decision making, they are especially pertinent in helping or hindering a person's movement through the contemplation stage.

*Interpersonal Relationships*
Interactions with key people in a person's life, such as spouses, partners, special friends, or lovers, can play a strong role when deciding to make or not make a change and in whether change is sustained over time.[4]

*Social Systems*
A person's family system, social network, work systems, or other societal systems may support or interfere with change. Families, in particular, can provide reasons for change or motivation to continue drinking or using; they can provide support for treatment and triggers for relapse.

*Enduring Personal Characteristics*
Basic personality characteristics also influence the change process. These might include attributes such as impulsiveness or compulsiveness, issues of personal identity, self-esteem, conscientiousness, extroversion, agreeableness, neuroticism, and so on. The effects of these characteristics can be seen in decision making, planning, perceptions, and implementation of an action plan.

■

Any of these areas of functioning may facilitate or complicate the process of change for any specific behavior, such as stopping the use of alcohol. Therefore, the big picture should be taken into account in assessing, planning, or supporting behavioral change. However, it's important not to let all the various considerations distract from the focus on the targeted change.

## Interaction of Dimensions

All four of these dimensions—stages of change, processes of change, markers of change, and context of change—interact with each other to form a complex picture of how people become addicted, how they heal from addiction, or how they alter other behaviors.

People generally do not move through the stages of change in a straightforward, linear way. They move through at different paces, some so quickly you have trouble identifying which stage they are in, and some over many years. They also move back and forth and re-cycle through the stages, which is discussed in the following section.

## Re-cycling

Most people have some trouble sustaining the changes, and relapse is the rule rather than the exception.[5] A relapse means a return to an earlier stage, sometimes all the way back to the precontemplation stage. Relapse also means more than a slip. It is a return to a pattern of prior behavior.

However, a relapse is not the same as failure. Relapse is a normal part of all kinds of change. Multiple attempts at change are common for any kind of change, from establishing new routines regarding medication compliance after a heart attack to following medication and diet regimens after a diagnosis of diabetes to quitting drug use. Most people travel through the stages of change several times before they attain success.[6] They use their experience in the process to adjust their plan for change, which in turn helps them be successful.

As people move through the stages of change another time, this time with more information and a better understanding than previously, they are actually re-cycling. They need to learn how to go through the stages better. They may discover that they have to change their environment in different or more ways than they had thought. They may discover that a certain goal was unrealistic. However, the relapse does not necessarily mean that the client does not want to change or cannot change.

TTM can be applied to many different behaviors and is most frequently applied to changes such as stopping smoking or drinking alcohol. The next chapter will look at how the transtheoretical model applies to the process of becoming addicted.

# 2

# The Movement into Addiction

We generally think of applying stages of change theory to people who are entering recovery or trying to alter a negative behavior. However, people go through the stages of change as they develop an addiction as well. Examining this process can help you understand how addictions are created and what needs to be undone in recovery. This chapter examines the four dimensions of change (stages, processes, markers, and context) in relation to developing an addiction.

## The Precontemplation Stage and Addiction

People in the precontemplation stage are not considering the addictive behavior. Their decisional balance—a marker of change—is negative. In other words, the negative aspects of drinking alcohol or using crack, for instance, clearly outweigh any potentially positive aspects. They have a high level of abstinence self-efficacy—another marker of change. That is, they feel sure they can abstain from use; they're not even tempted. Their context of change—their social and physical environment and their attitudes and beliefs—all support them in not using.

Generally, personal protective factors and lack of significant exposure will keep people in the precontemplation stage; that is, they will keep them from considering an addictive behavior. In some cases, people who are precontemplators simply don't know about the addictive behavior. This is probably the case with a very small proportion of persons when alcohol is being considered, but it may be a larger proportion when a designer drug such as Ecstasy is considered.

Even with some exposure, protective factors can keep the decisional balance negative. Well-known protective factors include religious involvement, good family relationships and interactions, good self-control or self-regulation skills, peers who are not using, parental monitoring, and economic and social stability.[1] These are all part of the context of change.

Let's look for a moment at how the processes of change interact with the context in this stage. You will remember that the internal processes of change are more relevant to the early stages of change. People whose context of change supports them to stay entirely away from drinking alcohol are apt to dismiss the idea of drinking when they are given information about it (consciousness raising) or are exposed to people who are drunk. They have few serious problems or issues that prompt them to reevaluate this thinking. They accept the norms that say trying an addictive behavior is unwise.

However, protective factors do not ensure that a person will remain in the precontemplation stage. Everyone is vulnerable to developing an addiction.

Is there a strategy that best keeps people from moving through the stages of change into addiction? Sometimes it may be best not to make an issue about the addictive behavior. But for high-risk youth or for any youth who will have easy accessibility or pressure to engage, it is probably better to move them into the contemplation stage so they can make a conscious decision not to use.

The processes of change that move people from precontemplation to contemplation with addictive behaviors are consciousness raising, environmental reevaluation, and self-reevaluation.

## The Contemplation Stage and Addiction

People are in the contemplation stage for starting an addictive behavior when they are open to considering the positive and negative aspects of the behavior. A transition to the contemplation stage happens primarily during adolescence, especially regarding alcohol and other drug use. This is a time when high-risk behaviors are particularly attractive.

It is often assumed that addictions begin automatically and involve little thought. However, in the contemplation stage, people start to actively think about using and the internal processes (cognitive and experiential) of change are engaged. Consciousness is raised as they listen to advertisements and stories, pay attention to role models to see how they deal with the behavior, check out what their peers are doing, and ask questions about consequences. They begin to evaluate both themselves and their environment. They compare the information they are getting to their own values and beliefs. They notice how the addictive behavior affects other people and how the people who are important to them feel about the behavior.

Movement through this stage can occur very slowly as people continue to notice and react to information or to their experience with the behavior. And so, information accumulates. They may remain in this stage for a long time, feeling ambivalent, moving back and forth between the pros and cons. They may ultimately move back into precontemplation or they may develop the personal rationale that will allow them to proceed toward addiction.

For example, a thirteen-year-old may hear a couple of his friends talking about how fun it was getting drunk. He may dismiss it as stupid. Over time he may be intrigued by a movie in which a character looks cool with a beer in his hand and a girl is attracted to him or a television show where several characters get "wasted" and have a lot of fun pulling silly antics. He compares things he's heard in drug education about the potential damage of alcohol with positive experiences friends relate. A year later he is at a party where he sees some guys he admires standing in the backyard passing a couple of beers and they invite him over. "Why not?" he thinks. "It can't hurt to try it."

Gathering information may include some experimental use; for some, especially if the experience is uncomfortable or frightening, the experiment can tip their decisional balance back toward precontemplation. However, if the experience is pleasurable or intriguing, it may move them toward continued experimentation. The adolescent with the beer may get a horrible hangover or lose driving privileges when his parents find out. In this case, he decides that the behavior is not worth it. On the other hand, he may get pleasantly tipsy and have other teens react to him as if he's really cool. He then decides this behavior has more positives than negatives. Or maybe it was LSD he tried, and he felt so out of control it frightened him, in which case he moved quickly back to precontemplation. Initial experimenters are best considered contemplators, but the first experience is often a critical element in the decisional balance that moves people forward through the stages or back into precontemplation.

The context of change brings many influences to bear on decision making in this stage. Protective factors include academic achievement, positive relationships with adults, prosocial attitudes and activities, self-confidence, and healthy peer networks. Risk factors include low self-esteem, problematic peers and relationships, and lack of achievement and prospects for success in life.

Peer or social influence is particularly important in tipping the decisional balance toward addiction. However, this influence passes "through the screen" of the person's knowledge, attitudes, and beliefs, as well as her personal experience.[2] For instance, the more negative a person's self-evaluation, the more susceptible he is to social influences.[3]

The person has moved into the preparation stage once she has progressed from the first experimental uses to an openness to use and repeated use.

## The Preparation Stage and Addiction

Experimentation increases during the preparation stage. The markers of change are pointing forward: the decisional balance is tipping toward more use; self-efficacy to abstain from the behavior diminishes as temptation increases.

Still, preparation is a transitional stage, and the verdict is out on which direction someone will take. A variety of influences interact to produce movement to the next stage, and they are difficult to isolate. All the processes of change come into play as physiology and psychology join together to influence use in this stage. The internal processes—consciousness raising, emotional arousal, self-reevaluation, environmental reevaluation, and social liberation—become connected to the behavioral processes of conditioning and reinforcement. More frequent experimentation means there are more cues in the environment that become associated with the addictive behavior. The behavior itself may give pleasure, the activities associated with the behavior may give pleasure, and both reinforce the desire to continue.

Add to this the context of change, which is interacting with the processes of change, and you have a very complicated picture. It is impossible to predict whether someone will move on to action or back to contemplation or even precontemplation. Still, looking at the possibilities can be useful.

It is in the preparation stage that multiple problems have their greatest influence. Someone who is faced with serious life problems and has low coping skills is more apt to find relief in addictive behaviors. Let's look at how the context of change plays out in the transition from preparation to action.

Remember that the context of change is divided into five aspects. The *current life situation* (environmental influences and psychological symptoms) has an important impact on the transition to the action stage. Someone who has a lot of anxiety or who has a group of friends who love to break rules will find the addictive behavior more useful. The person's *beliefs and attitudes* are significant as well. For instance, if a person belongs to a family that turns to pills to solve every problem or a family that is proud of its ability to drink, the person is more vulnerable to addiction. *Interpersonal relationships* also seem to have an enormous impact on addiction. These relationships are taken very seriously by adolescents in particular, and feelings of alienation from peers, conflicts with peers, and a sense of inadequate interpersonal skills can contribute significantly to addictive behavior. Conflicted or inadequate *social systems*, can also contribute to excessive use. Finally, *enduring personal characteristics,* such as problems with self-esteem and self-concept, influence initiation of addictive behaviors.[4]

The context of change, however, can offer protective factors as well. A youngster who, for instance, has a group of peers who do not drink alcohol or use other drugs, whose family models responsible use, and who has good interpersonal skills and strong self-esteem is less apt to move on to the action stage.

Still, the complexity of the interactions between the person and his environment make prediction impossible. For example, you could have two young women experimenting with cocaine who are very different and come from very different backgrounds, but both move from preparation to action. One young woman may have chronic trouble with schoolwork, have parents with serious marital problems who fight frequently in front of her, and hang out with older risk-taking friends who have gotten in trouble at school. The other young woman may be on the honor roll, have parents who get along well most of the time, and be involved in extracurricular activities, but have a problematic boyfriend. Both of these girls may experiment with cocaine and ultimately decide to repeat those experiments until the use becomes habitual.

### The Action and Maintenance Stages and Addiction

When people engage in an addictive behavior in a patterned, regular way, they have entered the action stage. They could be entering an action stage that will end in self-regulated, nonproblematic use. In such a case, excessive use and negative consequences will prompt self-reevaluation and lead to nonproblematic use, such as drinking beer or wine with meals but not to excess. These people ultimately enter a maintenance stage of self-regulated use.

For others, the action stage moves toward abuse and addiction. Abusers can remain in the action stage for long periods of time, with periods of problematic use interspersed with regulated use or abstinence. To be considered an addiction, the pattern of use is not only regular but also dependent. As defined in *Addiction and Change*, "The term *dependence* indicates that the pattern of behavior (1) is under poor self-regulatory control or appears out of control, (2) continues despite negative feedback, and (3) has become an integral part of the individual's life and coping."[5] These people are not dependent at the beginning of the action stage, but they engage in the processes of change in such a way that they move into addiction. In this framework, people are considered to be addicted when they have established a problematic pattern of use for at least three to six months. Once a problematic pattern is sustained and resistant to self-regulation, and once it meets the definition for dependence, the person moves into the maintenance stage.

In the action and maintenance stages, the internal processes of change are used to normalize the behavior and minimize problems. The person who is well into the action stage or in the maintenance stage of addiction uses a variety of tactics, or ways of thinking, to avoid making the connection, such as minimization, rationalization, projection, over-intellectualization, repression, and avoidance. Two of the most powerful tactics are deflection and disconnection. In deflection, the person attributes the consequence to a technical problem rather than to the addictive behavior. So when an alcoholic man gets arrested for driving under the influence (a DUI), the problem is that he got stopped by the police, not that he was drunk, and the solution is to be more vigilant for police. In disconnection, the person blames the consequence on a different factor. An alcoholic woman might blame certain problems in her marriage on her husband's hypersensitivity to drinking rather than on her drinking.

While the internal processes of change are engaged, the behavioral processes take precedence in the later stages of developing an addiction. Conditioning, stimulus generalization, and reinforcement connect the addictive behavior to the various areas of the person's life. Self-liberation (making behavioral choices and changes) and helping relationships (associating with people who support the addictive behavior) also play a critical role in creating the dependent pattern of use.

Addictive behaviors have a physiological and psychological reaction that are reinforcing: they are pleasurable. They take away pain, stress, and other negative emotions. This makes them vulnerable to conditioning; that is, the expectation of pleasure given by alcohol, other drugs, or other addictive behavior becomes paired with another cue. Seeing any white substance in a plastic bag prompts the same reaction as seeing cocaine. Hearing a certain song prompts the expectation of pleasure of smoking marijuana. The cue triggers a felt need for the substance or addictive behavior.

These physiological and psychological reactions also allow for stimulus generalization—expectations learned in one specific setting that are spread to other settings or circumstances. The behavior becomes paired with more parts of a person's life. A man drinks after work every Friday with colleagues, and he begins to have the same cocktail at home after work as well. Over time, simply coming home after work is paired with the expectation of drinking.

It's interesting to note that the setting for the behavior—the bar or the casino or the backyard—provide critical cues in the action stage. The bar with its bowl of beer nuts and appealing music or the casino without windows with cheap food or free drinks prompt and reinforce the addictive behavior. In contrast, in the maintenance stage, the behavior itself becomes so intrinsically rewarding that the settings have less influence.

Reinforcement works on many levels. There is the obvious reinforcement of the high itself, whether it's high emotional arousal, relaxation, or release of inhibitions. Reinforcement also takes subtler forms, such as release from tension, avoiding difficult emotions, easing self-doubt, and creating a sense of belonging. Eventually, the person can also experience the reinforcement of lifting the depression that follows the cocaine high or relieving the headache that follows alcohol intoxication.

The reinforcement value of the addictive behavior is especially strong when a person is turning to an addictive behavior to cope with negative emotions. The physiological effects are potent and can easily replace less quick or effective methods of coping. Research also shows that using addictive behavior to cope with negative emotions predicts movement toward abuse and dependence.[6] The person moves on toward addiction as she more often chooses the quick reinforcing effects of the addictive behavior over less immediately reinforcing coping activities.

While a person is responding to environmental and emotional cues that have been paired with use, he also continues to make choices. This is the process termed self-liberation—the process of making choices, whether healthy or not, and taking responsibility for the self. He makes choices to seek substances, to frequent the places where there is access, and to stay around people who engage in similar behaviors. There are virtually hundreds of little decisions made daily to ensure access to the behavior. It takes commitment to sustain this behavior when negative personal and social consequences begin to occur.

A person engages in the final behavioral process of change, helping relationships, as she associates increasingly with others who have similar behavior patterns. She uses this group as her measurement guide for herself so she can say, "I don't drink any more than my friends do. If I have a problem, so do all my friends!" The helping relationships in the context of becoming addicted allow people to rationalize and normalize their own behavior.

This is what movement through action into maintenance looks like: negative consequences that generally lead to reevaluation and self-regulation don't do so anymore. Generally, if you get a nasty hangover, you decide getting drunk isn't worth it. If you lose a hundred bucks, you decide gambling isn't worth it. But sometimes people don't experience significant negative consequences, or they minimize them. You got a nasty hangover, but it was a great night! That's what happens when you drink. You lost a hundred bucks, but what a thrill when you won the fifty bucks before that. It's worth another try.

As a person finds the addictive behavior reinforcing, he spends more time at it, and alternative behaviors and environments drop by the wayside. The world outside the addictive behavior shrinks; the world associated with the addictive behavior expands. The rewarding physiological effects of the behavior are paired with more and more situations and events. These persons only choose restaurants that serve liquor. The ball game is fun partly because of the beer. They accept an invitation from one couple over another because liquor will be available at one house.

As use progresses, the feedback system is co-opted. For instance, steady, heavy drinking is very likely to create problems in some arena of a person's life. While in the action stage, a person rationalized a hangover as the price she paid for fun. But as she moves into the maintenance phase, she may say she arrives habitually late to work not because of the hangovers, but because she is not a morning person. How people handle this feedback—whether they silence the information they get from the consequences or allow their consciousness to be raised—is critical in whether they move from abuse to addiction.

Now we'll look at how the context of change supports the movement into addiction. Remember that *enduring personal characteristics* and the *current life situation* (the emotional and mental status of the person) are two of the factors in the context of change. Several individual characteristics have been associated with addiction: disinhibition, impulsivity, or behavioral undercontrol.[7] In addition, people with chronic mental illnesses appear to be at a higher risk for developing an addiction. However, the risk for addiction does not lie in individual personality characteristics, but in their complex interaction with a variety of environmental and other factors.

Another factor of the context of change is *social systems* (family system, social network, work systems, or other societal systems). The family can influence movement toward addiction, particularly in adolescence, through reinforcement, lack of punishment, modeling, tacit approval, intense disapproval, and disengagement. It's a tough line to walk: the message for adolescents needs to be carefully crafted so it doesn't promote rebellion, and thus, movement toward addiction. Friendship networks also play a critical role. As people in the action stage move further toward addiction, they seek out and associate with networks that support use.

*Interpersonal relationships* (with important people such as spouses, partners, special friends, and lovers) is yet another factor in the context of change. A moderate user may move into abuse or addiction to accompany an alcohol-dependent partner or to cope with the negative feelings that result in the relationship. For adolescents, as they move out of the familial home, significant others become more influential.

The context of change is also shaped by the addictive behavior as relationships, beliefs, attitudes, and social systems are modified to support the person's use. As we saw in the earlier stages, multiple problems in the context of change encourage movement through the stages of change toward addiction. Once in the late action and the maintenance stages, the person will have developed multiple problems in his life context as a result of the addiction. Clinical depression, problematic expectations, marital conflict, and parental interference become reasons for sustaining the behavior. As researchers trying to understand the development of addictions have found, "Life problems promote engagement in the addictive behavior, which in turn increases the number and intensity of life problems, which promotes engagement in the addictive behavior. . . ."[8]

In the action and maintenance stages of addiction, the

decisional balance is decisively weighted in favor of the addictive behavior. There are real positives for the person, especially when considerations such as avoiding withdrawal begin to kick in. At the same time, the often-serious negative consequences do not weigh in heavily. People in the latter parts of the action stage and in the maintenance stage of addiction engage the internal change process of self-reevaluation to maintain this decisional balance. They reorganize how they see the behavior in terms of their current values and beliefs, and in this case, it is in the service of keeping the valued addiction.

You will remember that another marker of change is self-efficacy—a person's confidence that she can perform a certain behavior. In these stages of change, people have an overinflated sense of self-efficacy. They are sure they can control the behavior if they want to. In other words, their self-assessment is no longer accurate and helps explain why the basic feedback of negative consequences fails in these stages.

■

Just as people move through all five stages of change in developing an addiction, they also move through all five stages when recovering. In the final two chapters, we will look at how people move through the stages of change as they recover from an addiction. Chapter 3 looks at the characteristics of people in recovery as they occupy each of the five stages of change. Understanding this helps you assess where a client is at in the larger process of change. Chapter 4 looks at how people engage in the process of change during recovery and how the context of change supports them. This knowledge aids you in helping clients engage the processes of change.

# 3

# Making an Assessment

As people recover from an addiction, they move through the same five stages of change as they did when they developed the addiction. It is something like a mirror image. If they were not even entertaining the idea of drinking when they were in precontemplation for addiction, now in precontemplation for recovery, they are not even entertaining the idea of stopping their drinking or other drug use.

Identifying a client's stage of change in treatment planning is essential for a clinician. However, this can be complicated because people don't always fall neatly into one category or another. This is in part because people may be in different stages for different substances or addictive behaviors. For instance, a person might be in the action stage of recovery for a smoking addiction, the preparation stage of recovery for alcohol addiction, and in the precontemplation stage of recovery for a marijuana addiction.

It can also be complicated because people's behavior may be misleading. A person may have stopped using entirely, leading you to think he's in action. However, he's stopped only to prove to somebody else that he doesn't have a problem. He doesn't believe for a second that he really has a problem. Thus it's very important to examine thoughts, attitudes, and behaviors together to see if behavior is consistent with attitudes and thoughts.

So how do you make an assessment? You must first be able to recognize the behaviors and attitudes of each stage. The kinds of things to look for are the following:
- Have they made any changes?
- Are they working to get the addiction back under control?
- Have they modified their behavior?
- Do they consider this a serious problem that needs to be changed?
- How important is it to them?
- How confident are they that they can make the change?

This chapter looks first at the characteristics of each stage of change for people in recovery, and then at how you determine what stage they are in.

## What to Look for in Each Stage

### *Precontemplation*
In this stage, you look for what people are *not* doing. They are not engaging in any of the processes of change. They are not abstaining or cutting back or creating a plan to do so. They are not even thinking about it. They are not comparing their addictive behavior to their values or looking at the impact of their behavior on others. At least that's usually the case. You may find, as noted previously, that people will sometimes quit using to please another person, but they're still not engaging in any processes of change. It is external compliance only.

What they *are* doing is minimizing the impact of their substance use and rationalizing their behavior. These people believe personally and deeply in their rationales, which are, in fact, strategies that keep them in precontemplation. The strategies used by people in precontemplation tend to fall into five categories:

1. *Reveling.* The addictive behavior is just too much fun to consider change. A person using this strategy focuses on how good the highs are or how "fine" the substance is.
2. *Reluctance.* Change would mean disruption, and it just isn't worth it. A person in this position may tell herself, "Everyone has one bad habit." Inertia, rather than energy, characterizes this strategy.
3. *Rebellion.* The right to use is a mark of freedom. People who fit this label are characterized by lots of energy and passion about the right to make their own decisions. They are resentful about anyone telling them what to do.
4. *Resignation.* It's hopeless. These people are overwhelmed by their problems, including the addictive behavior, and they feel helpless. You may hear, "Nothing really works for me."
5. *Rationalizing.* There are good reasons why the addictive behavior is not a problem. In contrast to people who are resigned, people who are rationalizing appear to have all the answers: "I rarely go above the limit I set for myself" or "I'll stop when I have kids." It's easy to get in a debate with people who engage in this strategy.[1]

*Contemplation*

People in the contemplation stage are starting to think about change. However, the stage is marked by ambivalence. You hear many qualifiers: "I should really do something, but . . ." or "Marijuana is causing some problems, but . . ."

In TTM model language, they are beginning to engage the internal (cognitive and experiential) processes of change. They are able to hear some feedback and are beginning to use the information they receive to compare their behavior with their own values and consider its impact on those around them. They are weighing the pros and cons of the addictive behavior. But the pros are still winning. You will remember that one of the markers of change is decisional balance, which indicates, in that person's opinion, whether the benefits of changing outweigh the costs of changing. In the contemplation stage, people's decisional balance is moving, but still tipping back and forth between using or not. The contemplation stage doesn't end until the decisional balance has tipped far enough that they can make a decision to do something. You do not see many behavior changes in this stage.

***Preparation***

People in the preparation stage often look anxious and hesitant, but they also look like they're ready to make a try at changing. They know they need to do something, and they have decided to do something. Now they need to figure out what to do and how much energy and commitment they are going to put toward doing this. You will often see people in this stage beginning to take small steps to change their behavior. They may be trying to cut back, spending more time at home with the family, putting more energy into school activities, asking for some feedback, or not stopping for a drink after work with their buddies. They are working on building a plan for change.

They are blending the internal processes of change with an initial foray into the external, behavioral processes. They're still thinking, but they're also beginning to take some responsibility for their choices. They're still weighing pros and cons, noticing how their behavior affects other people, but they are also engaging in stimulus control (not stopping at the bar) and counterconditioning (participating in competing activities at school) as they plan for a more complete change. You will see the decisional balance tipping further toward quitting the addiction as the pros for change start to win out, as they make a firm decision, and as they begin to gain confidence that they can do it (self-efficacy). They outline things they will do or steps they will take in the near future.

*Action*

The action and maintenance stages are the easiest to identify. There is a marked and visible change when people enter the action stage. Their thoughts and behavior are consistent. They are not only talking the talk, but they're also walking the walk.

People are engaging the behavioral processes of change in order to "break their habit." They may be attending AA (helping relationships), earning and asking for medallions (reinforcement), avoiding the bar entirely and being wary of social situations where there will be a lot of drinking (stimulus control), spending their evenings at home, or participating in weekend activities that don't include alcohol or other drugs (counterconditioning). They talk about what's hard and what's not, and what's working and what isn't. They experience pleasure in their victories, and self-efficacy grows. As their confidence increases, the temptation they experience decreases.

*Maintenance*

People in maintenance are integrating sober behaviors into their life. They still have to monitor addiction cues and triggers, and may sometimes long for the addictive behaviors, but they know clearly that the cons of the addictive behavior outweigh the pros. They don't feel a lot of temptation to use or engage in other addictive behaviors in most places or situations, and they are fairly confident in their ability to maintain sobriety.

As people remain in maintenance and solidify this stage, they use the experiential and behavioral processes of change less and less. They don't have to keep weighing the pros and cons as much. They aren't constantly evaluating themselves or the impact of their behavior on others. They don't need to monitor cues or triggers or worry about planning alternative activities. They just have to watch out for the infrequent trigger. This is a good time for a counselor to suggest regular "checkups," in a similar way to seeing a dentist every six months.

### How Do You Make the Assessment?

While there are a variety of tools available to use in identifying a person's stage of change, you will basically be looking for the characteristics that define each stage. This entails careful consideration of both attitudes and behavior, and a consideration of whether the attitudes and behavior are congruent. People's behavior may suggest they are in the action stage, but their thoughts and attitudes reveal that they are in an earlier stage. For instance, a woman may have stopped an addictive behavior only to prove she does not have a problem. Or a man may say he knows he has a problem with gambling and has stopped betting on baseball, but he still goes to the track regularly. He is not doing the kinds of things that would move him out of betting. People can fool you with the way they talk and behave. Thus, it is very important to look at both the behavior and the thinking.

It's also important to consider the markers for change—decisional balance and self-efficacy/temptation. Assessing decisional balance is especially helpful in identifying the early stages. Self-efficacy—the belief that they can do a certain task and have some control over events—begins to increase in the preparation stage and grows markedly as they go into action and maintenance. Self-efficacy is not a global measure like

## What You May Hear during Each Stage of Change[2]

1. Precontemplation (not seeing a problem)
   - "I don't have a drinking problem."
   - "I don't see that I need to change anything. All my friends get high a couple times a week. It's normal."
   - "I'm more creative when I smoke marijuana."
   - "I can't quit. I've tried a hundred times before. I just can't do it."

2. Contemplation (considering change)
   - "I worry sometimes about the amount I'm drinking, but then I look at my friends and I see they're drinking more than I am."
   - "I think my husband might be right, that I'm risking too much money at the casino. But then I think, I don't lose much more there than we might spend on other kinds of entertainment."

3. Preparation (deciding how to change)
   - "I really need to stop drinking. It's hurting my family."
   - "Tell me what treatment is like."

4. Action (making the change)
   - "I feel so good about what I'm doing. It's not that I wake up in the morning and think it's a piece of cake. It's still hard sometimes, but I have a lot more confidence that I can do this."

5. Maintenance (sticking with it)
   - "I like the way my life is. I don't want to go back to using."
   - "I am totally committed to sobriety. I know I could slip, because I have. If I start feeling upset or anxious about something, I know it's time to figure out what's bothering me, because I like the sober life."
   - "I haven't had a drink for months, but I still get the urge."

self-esteem. It is specific to certain behaviors or situations and has to be assessed in relation to those.

The assessment of stage is a continuous process. People move through stages at different rates, and move backward and forward as well. They can slip back to an earlier stage from week to week or day to day. Sometimes movement forward or backward even occurs within a session. You will want to do a stage status assessment frequently. It can be useful to do a sensitive assessment of stage at the beginning of each session.

Assessment tools range from clinical interviews to formal measurement instruments. The formal measurement instruments are more useful for research or for clinics tracking whole populations. This manual focuses more on clinical assessments.

***Clinical Interview***

Assessment requires being very sensitive to the client. It is crucial that you listen closely and perceptively, hearing the client's thoughts, feelings, and beliefs. It is easy to bring your own values into the treatment room in such a way that they color what you hear from the client. Do you think it's important to be at all of a child's soccer games, but the client puts much more value on other parts of her relationship with her child? Do you believe shouting is disrespectful, but the client sees it as a normal expression of strong feelings? If you are to understand where the client is, you have to recognize both your personal and cultural biases.

*Understanding Other Cultures*

It is critical to be aware and respectful of the customs and values that characterize various ethnic and racial groups. This can range from an understanding of the customs and traditions of a population group to the deeply held values that inform the culture.

According to Navajo custom, for example, when first introduced, a person generally expects to say his name, clan relationship or ethnic origin, and place of origin. Physical contact is minimal, and even a brief handshake may be no more than a soft touch of the palms.[3] Traditional Hmong avoid eye contact and women do not shake hands with each other or with men. Some cultural groups will feel most comfortable talking over a meal, and some will expect the clinician to answer some personal questions about herself that locate her in the world.

Deeply held values may differ as well. Some cultures will emphasize deference to elders or stronger connections with extended family than other cultures. Some cultures will be oriented toward the primacy of the community, while others, including mainstream American culture, emphasize the person's individual rights and desires. For example, African American clients may tend to understand substance use not solely as an individual phenomenon. They may see it within the context of historical and systemic forces of oppression and racism. The adverse effects of substance use are considered to negatively affect the community, as well as the individual. A person's healing represents a healing of the community.[4]

Much has been written about cultural competence in counseling in recent years, and there are a wide variety of resources available.[5]

---

A clinician must avoid biased assumptions, quick impressions, or poor listening to accurately identify a stage of change. You need to be open to the client to really understand where he is coming from. Without this, you can't engage people on an authentic level, and consequently you can't help them integrate changes into their life. Real change only occurs when they change for their own reasons. Good interviews that can also be motivational include the following four elements:

1. *Listening.* You can ask questions, of course, but not too many. Invite the client to talk, allow her time, and listen attentively and appreciatively. Don't bombard the client with questions or make quick decisions about her answers. Careful and open listening to the client's thought process while you observe her demeanor is the most productive way to assess client status.

2. *Ask probing, open-ended questions.* Closed-ended questions (ones that can be answered with a yes or no, such as "Did you drink?") or directive questions ("You're still feeling confident, aren't you?") give you limited information. Open-ended questions ("How did things go for you this week with your drinking?") are more apt to elicit information and feelings and help you to understand where the client really is.

3. *Checking your perceptions.* Check in with the client periodically to see if you are getting it right. You can summarize in your own words what you heard the client say and ask if you understood correctly. You can clarify, asking if this is what he means. This helps to ensure you understand client intentions and meanings.

4. *Reviewing stage status regularly.* You may wish to review stage status at the end of a session, as well as at the beginning, but in any case, do so regularly. Be sensitive to movement in either direction. Identifying stage status is at the heart of matching techniques to client needs.

## Measurement Techniques and Tools

There are some simple techniques and tools to help you as you identify the behaviors and attitudes that characterize each stage. Of course, these assessment techniques also prompt thoughts and feelings in the clients, and so may also begin to effect change in them.

### Rulers

Rulers can help you probe people's stage of change. This is as simple as asking people where they are on a scale of one to ten. For instance, with the Readiness Ruler (see exercise 1 on page 87 in appendix E), developed by Stephen Rollnick, you simply ask people to rate their own readiness to change.[6] The lower the number, the less ready they are to change. You can adapt this ruler to assess a variety of questions such as "How confident are you that you won't use?" or "How tempted are you to drink on a day-to-day basis?" or "How committed are you to making this change?"

### Description of a Typical Day

This indirect technique helps build rapport and raise consciousness while it gives you information. You ask clients to talk about a typical day from beginning to end. Follow them through the sequence of an entire day. Keep asking what happens, focusing on both feelings and behaviors. Avoid any reference to "problems" or "concerns," and avoid interjecting any opinions.

This technique opens up a conversation and you can learn a great deal about what the behavior means to clients and how hard it may be to give it up. It can tell you if substance use is the most cohesive element in their lives and give information on what drives the use—powerful cravings, emotional wounds, excitement, or other motivations.[7] This technique is most helpful perhaps in the contemplation stage, but it's also helpful in preparation and action since it gives information on how people are tempted as they go about their day.

*Decisional Balance Exercises*

A very simple pro and con exercise can be used with clients to help both you and them understand what stage of change they are in. Make a copy of Exercise 2: Decisional Balance Worksheet on page 89 in appendix E. You can either ask your client to fill in the worksheet or fill it out together as you discuss it.

Clients might, for example, write under the pros column for continuing behavior: "Drinking helps me have fun and socialize," "It helps me to loosen up," "It helps me fall asleep," and "It takes the edge off." Under the cons column, they might write "It's causing problems," "I have to lie to my wife," and "My husband is disappointed in me when I drink." Both you and your client can then see whether or not the benefits outweigh the costs. Note that it's possible that there are more pros for change than cons, but that the personal value of one con could be so significant to the individual that it outweighs several pros.

There are also a variety of scales people have developed that allow clients to identify pros and cons of using alcohol and other drugs, which are then used for evaluation. A formal instrument may help explore the issue more thoroughly because it identifies a wide variety of possible pros and cons for people. The answers are scored and can be used to give people feedback about themselves. In the Alcohol (and Illegal Drugs) Decisional Balance Scale, respondents indicate on a five-point scale how important each statement is in making a decision to change their behavior. See appendix A for a reproducible copy of this scale and for source information.

*Self-Efficacy and Temptation Measures*

As alluded to earlier, the ruler can be used to assess people's self-efficacy with questions about confidence and temptation. Generally, people's experience of temptation decreases as their confidence to abstain increases. However, this is not always the case. People can be very tempted and confident that they can abstain at the same time. Examples of statements you will be looking for as indicators of self-efficacy level include the following: "It won't be easy, but I can do this," "I think it's possible," "I'm afraid I can't do it," and "It's too overwhelming for me."

You can also look at self-efficacy and temptation in specific situations. The Brief Situational Confidence Questionnaire (BSCQ) asks people to identify their level of confidence to resist drinking in eight types of situations. It is a shorter version of the one-hundred–item Situational Confidence Questionnaire (SCQ) and is easier to use in clinical practice. With only eight items, the BSCQ can be administered in a few minutes and is easily interpreted by clinicians. A 1996 study found that the shorter version was effective and corresponded well with the longer version on most subscales.[8] See appendix B for more information on this questionnaire.

The Alcohol Abstinence Self-Efficacy Scale (AASE) is also easy to use and has been found to have strong indices of reliability and validity.[9] The instrument consists of twenty items and can be used to assess both the temptation to drink and the confidence to abstain. People rate temptation and confidence on separate five-point Likert scales. The scores measure four types of situations in which people are most likely to be overwhelmed by temptation. In decreasing order of importance, they are (1) negative emotional states such as anger, depression, or frustration; (2) social pressures such as celebrating with a group of people who are drinking; (3) withdrawal symptoms and urges or cravings; and (4) physical or other concerns, such as being worried about someone or persistent pain. Additional information on this instrument, which is in the public domain, can be found in appendix C.

The University of Rhode Island Change Assessment Scale (URICA) is a scale that consists of thirty-two items that reflect four stages of change: precontemplation, contemplation, action, and maintenance. People rate agreement or disagreement with statements on a five-point Likert scale. People can be assigned a score for each of the stages of change. There are also short forms of the URICA. While this instrument is an excellent way to measure stages of change with substance-abusing clients, it requires scoring and comparison with norms and is best used in a setting where statistical expertise is available. Additional information on this instrument, which is also in the public domain, can be found in appendix D.

### Assessment with Special Populations

Certain populations present unique challenges in assessment. Among these are people who are not currently engaging in the addictive behavior, but at the same time are not necessarily in the action stage.

Pregnant women sometimes stop smoking to avoid harming their unborn children. This does not necessarily mean they intend to stop permanently. People who are receiving inpatient treatment in hospitals or who are in prison cannot move beyond the preparation stage because they have no opportunity to engage in the behavior. People in these settings may be confident, but their ability to abstain is guaranteed by external sources. Thus, they have to be evaluated differently than people who have access to substances.

Another population that presents unique assessment challenges is those with co-occurring disorders. It is common to find that people who are addicted to substances also have depression, anxiety, or other mood disorders. You may suspect or determine the presence of these disorders as the result of your clinical interview. If you are in doubt, there are also screening instruments for mood disorders. SAMHSA's *TIP 9: Assessment and Treatment of Patients with Coexisting Mental Illness and Alcohol and Other Drug Use* provides practical and useful treatment recommendations for enhancing services to dually diagnosed people with mental health and substance abuse problems.[10]

Co-occurring disorders make treatment more complex and they should generally be addressed at certain points in the treatment or therapy process. For instance, sometimes people cannot move beyond the contemplation stage if their depression is too severe, and the depression will have to be addressed simultaneously with the addiction. However, it is important to not lose focus on the addiction itself.

■

In summary, you as a clinician need to identify your clients' stage of change in recovery in order to best help them engage in the processes of change. Assessing the stage of change requires observing or eliciting information about the clients' attitudes and behaviors and determining which stage they reflect. The clinical interview is the most frequently used tool in a clinical setting. There are some additional short, easy-to-use tools as well. Information on several such assessment tools can be found in the appendixes. Finally, there are more elaborate assessment tools that are useful in research or evaluation of larger populations.

Once you have an understanding of where in the stages of recovery the client is at present, you can focus on how to help him make progress toward sustained change. The strategies you use will depend on the stage of change.

# 4

# Practical Strategies for Helping People in Recovery

People who are recovering from an addiction must engage in specific processes of change in order to complete the tasks that allow them to move on to the next stage of change in their recovery. Once you've identified the stage a client is in, you can understand the processes that could help him progress through the stages. In other words, knowing a client's stage of change helps you determine what kinds of strategies may be useful at a particular time.

In this section we will look at the tasks and goal for each stage of change, and then at the kinds of strategies and techniques you can use to help people do what they need to do to move into the next stage. In TTM language, you can help them engage in change processes that will enable them to move forward.

### Precontemplation

*Tasks:* Increase awareness that there is a problem and a need to change.

Envision the possibility of change.

*Goal:* Give serious consideration to changing this behavior.

*Processes of Change:*   The cognitive/experiential (internal) processes of consciousness raising and emotional arousal raise awareness of a problem, and self-reevaluation and environmental reevaluation create dissonance between the addictive behavior and the person's values.

---

Because people who are in precontemplation are not thinking at all about changing, they pose a particular challenge to the clinicians who are working with them. They are engaging in strategies that help them stay in the precontemplation stage despite the fact that their addictive behaviors are causing unpleasant consequences. The assessment chapter reviewed strategies people use to keep from thinking about changing (reveling, reluctance, rebellion, resignation, and rationalizing). It's challenging to talk to clients about a need to change without prompting them to engage in one of these holding strategies.

The goal is to help them realize that there is a problem and a need to change without raising their defenses. So in the precontemplation stage (and the contemplation stage to some extent), what you don't do is as important as what you do do. Don't confront. Don't judge. Don't label. This kind of feedback risks making the problem worse. The old medical adage "First do no harm" is relevant here. Evidence suggests that confrontational feedback generally provokes resistance and more denial;[1] it risks driving a wedge between the clinician and the client.

The question then becomes "How do you help someone get motivated without creating resistance and more denial?" The answer: by creating an accepting, understanding atmosphere where people can explore any slight concern about the addictive behavior or slight ambivalence about change. An empathetic atmosphere allows for a sensitive view into the person and a deeper understanding of how she truly views her own situation and behavior. The stages of change model recognizes lack of concern and motivation to consider change as the first part of the process of change. The challenge is to help people become motivated. They become motivated by becoming aware that there is a problem and by experiencing some internal discomfort. Awareness can begin in the form of unpleasant consequences (although very severe consequences can also increase people's sense of hopelessness or result in more substance use to relieve the stress and stop the pain). Awareness can also begin in mandatory treatment. However, it does not always happen even there. Ultimately, movement to the next stage depends on the client's motivation to change, not just to avoid negative consequences or please somebody else. It's critical to elicit the client's real feelings and beliefs about his behavior.

In TTM language, the change processes in which the person engages are the internal processes, particularly consciousness raising, emotional arousal, self-reevaluation, and environmental reevaluation.

## *Motivational Interviewing*

Finding and increasing motivation are at the heart of change in the precontemplation and contemplation stages. Enhancing motivation is also at the heart of the therapeutic approach called motivational interviewing (MI). This approach, developed by William Miller and Stephen Rollnick in 1991, is an excellent match for working with clients in the early stages of change.[2]

Motivational interviewing is a philosophical approach in which the clinician is an empathic partner who works collaboratively with the client. It's important that the clinician understand the MI style and its techniques. The MI style seeks to accept, empower, support, and understand clients. MI incorporates many basic counseling skills such as use of open-ended questions, careful and active listening, affirming clients, reflecting, and summarizing. These counseling skills are employed to help the clients achieve the tasks that will help them move into the next stage of change. So the counseling skills are both empathic and directive.

Highlighting discrepancies between goals and behaviors is an important part of motivational interviewing. If a client's task is to become aware of the problems associated with her addictive behavior and the need to change, it is critical to discover the discrepancy between where she is and where she wants to be.

However, you will want to elicit *the client's* values, concerns, and issues regarding this particular behavior. It is critical to remain aware that your values are not the important ones here. It is tempting to try to convince clients about what you feel is important. When you can clearly see the reasons why they should change, it can seem like you ought to be able to just tell them. But your reasons are not good enough. It does not matter if it is clear to you; it only matters if it is clear to your client.

Eliciting values, concerns, and issues may begin with techniques such as exploring the meaning of events that brought the client to treatment and eliciting the client's perceptions of the problem. What are his goals and expectations that may be problematic for him at this point? He may be disappointed that he hasn't been able to build the career he had hoped to build or establish a successful marriage and family. If he can begin to become aware of the differences between what he hoped for himself and his current situation, if he can begin to experience at a conscious level some internal discomfort, he will gain some motivation to change.

Another MI technique that is appropriate for this stage

is providing information and feedback. There are two essential aspects to giving this feedback. First, the feedback must be personalized, that is, based on information you have gathered through forms that clients have filled out and/or through talking with them. Second, the feedback must be objective. Thus, the emphasis is not on what clients are doing wrong, but on how their behavior differs from the norm and what risks are associated with it. You will want to compare clients' specific information with normative information. For instance, you may talk about how the amount of drinking a woman does in a given week or month compares to national averages for women her age. As you give this feedback, you can also talk about the risk factors associated with her level of drinking or other addictive behavior and about the kinds of problems that can be associated with it.

You may also want to give amplified feedback to a person who is totally happy with his addictive behavior. Suppose he says, "Drinking is no problem for me. Yeah, I suppose it causes trouble once in a while, but it's worth it. I'm the kind of guy who just really likes to have a good time." You might exaggerate a bit, saying something such as, "So you think this is the most important thing in your life?" At the same time, remember that you must remain sincere. Clients will quickly pick up if you are playing games with them.

This, of course, is only the barest sketch of motivational interviewing. There are additional MI techniques that are useful, such as rolling with resistance, in which you join with the client and explore rather than confront resistance; and double-sided reflection, which directs clients back to their ambivalence. Anyone wishing to practice this approach should investigate it in more depth. Valuable resources include *Motivational Interviewing: Preparing People for Change* by William Miller and Stephen Rollnick and *Motivational Interviewing and Stages of Change* by Kathyleen Tomlin and Helen Richardson.[3]

**Values Clarification**

Values clarification exercises can also help to raise consciousness and prompt clients to engage in self-reevaluation. Asking clients to talk about what is important to them can be the first step in looking at whether their choices are consistent with these values. As an additional aid, you might make cards with values listed on them—my family, my children, my career, my friends, sports, adventure, having fun, making money, helping others, making a difference in the world—and ask your client to sort them, arranging the values by highest priority.

Next, of course, is to guide your clients in observations about whether their behavior is consistent with these values. You might mention that it seems using alcohol or other drugs is a very important behavior to them. Through open-ended, exploratory questions and careful reflection of their answers, you help them see what a central value their addictive behavior has in their lives.

**AA Meetings**

Sending people to AA meetings just to listen can prompt people to think about how their behavior compares to that of others. Ask them to come back and talk about how they are, or are not, different than the other people in the meeting. Process the activity with them. You might ask questions such as, "Was there anybody there who is like you, anybody that you could identify with?" "How were they like you?" "How were they different?" "How was what they talked about experiencing different from what you're experiencing?" "Did anybody receive a medallion?" and "What did you think about that?" The AA meeting becomes a probe, an opportunity for people to reflect on themselves in relation to this experience.

## Experiential Techniques

Using experiential techniques can be especially helpful in emotional arousal. For instance, you might ask a client to role-play a situation in which there could be an unsettling consequence of the addictive behavior, perhaps facing her daughter the day after a party in which she got drunk and did something embarrassing. Or you might ask a client to assume the role of his parent or wife or another significant person in his life when he has just driven home from the bar and is slurring his words. This can raise awareness and emotional intensity at the same time.

## Including a Significant Other

Sometimes it is helpful to bring a significant other into a session to help support the client's motivation. She can tell her partner about problematic effects she has noticed and how the addictive behavior has affected her, and she can provide support for change. However, this technique must be handled very carefully. If the significant other comes to the session angry and accusatory, it could, like a clinician's confrontational feedback, backfire. You will need to determine first whether the significant other has a positive relationship with the client and an investment in contributing to the change process. If so, you can elicit supportive statements with questions such as "Have you noticed the efforts he has made to change his drinking?" and "What is different now that leads you to feel better about his ability to change?"[4]

## Looking down the Road

Asking people to project themselves into the future is a motivational interviewing technique that is useful in helping people envision the possibility of change. Ask your client how she sees herself three months from now without making any changes. Ask her how it would look to her three months from now if she did make some changes. Or a year from now, or three years from now. Ask what she would see herself doing, and what her life would look like.

***Cautions***

- Offering advice or telling people what to do are apt to provoke resistance.
- Giving significant action assignments will be counterproductive at this stage. If people are not ready to take action, they are apt to move in the opposite direction.
- Offering a lot of choices may overwhelm clients at this stage. It is a time to move gently and slowly.
- Use of medications to address the addiction in this stage is problematic. Clients may sabotage a medication's effectiveness if they are not ready for it, and then may believe that no medication can ever be helpful.
- Sometimes it is necessary to address life problems, such as dual diagnoses or severe environmental stressors, even in this early stage.

■

The precontemplation focus is to help the client become aware that a problem exists. As a clinician, you cannot make a person get motivated, and frontal attacks are apt to backfire. However, you can cultivate seeds of doubt. You are most apt to nurture awareness in a client by accepting him, by eliciting his perspectives and feelings, and by openly discussing the addictive behavior and its consequences.

## Contemplation

| | |
|---|---|
| *Tasks:* | Consider the costs and benefits of quitting in order to make a firm decision to quit or modify the behavior. |
| | Make a decision. |
| *Goal:* | Complete a considered evaluation that leads to a decision to change. |
| *Processes of Change:* | The internal processes of consciousness raising, emotional arousal, self-reevaluation, and environmental reevaluation continue to increase awareness of problems and dissonance. Social liberation prompts recognition that others in society encourage the behavior change. |

People enter this stage with some awareness of a need for change, but with more cons than pros for change. Before they can move to the next stage, the decisional balance must be tipped in the other direction. This means helping them to thoroughly consider the costs and benefits of their behavior. Contemplation, or careful consideration, is particularly difficult for people who are addicted. They tend to be impulsive and seek immediate gratification. This, of course, makes it difficult for them to reach a decision, which is the goal of this stage. They are prone to rush into a decision before they have an understanding of what the change may entail or to procrastinate, get stuck in their ambivalence, and stay in this stage for a long time.

One of the most important functions for the clinician who is working with someone in contemplation is to help the client deal with the ambivalence that is the hallmark of this stage. The focus of the work becomes assisting the client in attaining clarity on the benefits of maintaining the addictive behavior versus changing the behavior, both on a cognitive and emotional level. The same internal change processes that are important in precontemplation continue to be engaged in, but they go beyond raising awareness of the problem. The emphasis is more on self-reevaluation and social liberation, in which the client accepts the negative societal value about the particular addictive behavior.

Motivational interviewing techniques continue to be very useful. This includes continuing to provide objective feedback in an open, attentive, and concerned atmosphere and helping the person to explore thoughts and behavior by asking probing, open-ended questions. Cultural sensitivity, as was discussed in chapter 3, is also particularly important here. A client will need to both feel and be understood if she is going to make the decision her own.

### *Risk/Reward Analysis*

The Decisional Balance Worksheet discussed in chapter 3 is also an intervention tool. When you are using this exercise, be aware that while reasoning is important in analyzing risks and rewards, such an analysis is much more than that. Thus, cognitive-behavioral techniques can be important, and so can insight-oriented and experiential techniques when examining risks and rewards.

Remember, a person's feelings about any particular pro or con are what give it weight. A mother's feeling about her child's disappointment in her may outweigh the social lubricant, relaxation, and diversion functions of alcohol. Many of the emotionally arousing interventions will occur outside sessions and can be explored in the session as the person introduces them. You might also ask clients to imagine past events that resulted in painful consequences or to relive old parental or familial events marred by addictive behavior. Psychodrama and other experiential techniques can help make the pros and cons more vivid and powerful.

Bring to light *all* your client's considerations for and against change. People who are addicted frequently rush to make a long list of points against maintaining the addiction. They may want to please you; they may want to convince themselves and hope that the weight of the list will make them change. But focusing only on the negative aspects of the behavior leaves them bewildered about why it is so difficult for them to change. Acknowledging the pros for maintaining the addiction increases their awareness of the extent of the problem and helps them understand the power of its attraction for them and the level of commitment they will need in order to stop the behavior. An accurate evaluation of the role that the addictive behavior plays in their life seems to be important for fostering a serious decision to change.

### *Self-Monitoring*

Self-monitoring raises awareness and provides important information for the planning that takes place in the next stage. Ask people to track the frequency, amounts, and situations surrounding their use of alcohol, other drugs, or other addictive behavior. Many times people will carry a notepad and mark down, for instance, when they smoked a cigarette, what they were doing at the time, and how strongly they wanted the cigarette. They can do the same with drinking alcohol. People are frequently surprised by what they learn about their use in this process. Ask them to notice what they were doing when they took the first drink, what was going on that got them to the second drink, and so on. The typical-day exercise discussed on page 39 of chapter 3 is a self-monitoring tool that can be used within a session.

### *Role Modeling and Helping Relationships*

AA meetings can offer people role models that influence their perception of social norms (the social liberation change process) and engage them in helping relationships. The meetings also offer models of people who may have been successful, people who were like them. It can help them see what life might be like if they're able to move through this process of change.

Another strategy that can be helpful is to ask subgroups of addicted individuals to attend AA meetings attended by others who are similar to them. For instance, ask a doctor to go to a meeting where they will find other doctors or blue-collar workers to attend a meeting where they will find other blue-collar workers. Seeing and listening to colleagues and co-workers makes it more difficult to avoid making comparisons to themselves.

## *Sobriety Sampling*

Sobriety sampling—abstaining for a limited period of time—allows people to experiment with the new behavior of abstinence. This is the reverse of the experimentation that takes place in the contemplation stage when people are developing an addiction. A clinician might say, "I know you don't want to quit yet, and you're not sure you really want to, but can you try to go just one day without a drink?" Or perhaps ask for one week.

A small sample of sobriety can give them important information in this stage. Some people will say, "Wow, that was easier than I thought it would be." Some will find it harder than they thought. Some will discover that they start drinking earlier in the day than they had realized. If your client is among those who says, "Wow, that was harder than I thought it would be," you can observe that he is going to need lots of assistance to be successful making the change. To provide encouragement, add that there is help available for him to add to his list of pros for making the change.

## A Moral Inventory

Assigning various Steps in the Twelve Step facilitation process can be useful at different stages. In this stage, the Fourth Step of making a "searching and fearless moral inventory" helps people notice the effects of their behavior on others. In TTM language, this helps the client to engage in the change process called environmental reevaluation and can be a very important strategy in helping people tip the decisional balance toward change.

## Addressing Other Life Problems as Leverage

In the context of change, you will frequently find there are many complications attending the life of the person who is addicted. People may come to your office as a consequence of their use, but be more willing to talk about their marital or job problems. The marriage or job problems can then be used as leverage to prompt them to look at changing their addictive behavior. The problem they are willing to talk about is a good place to start, but always return to the addictive behavior. You might ask, "Do you think the problems you're talking about with your job could have anything to do with the way you use alcohol?" Connect the problems they raise back to their addictive behavior as frequently as you can, using a questioning manner or tone.

■

The contemplation stage requires a thorough and deep exploration of the costs and benefits of both continuing the addictive behavior and of changing. This is done on both a cognitive and an emotional level. It is as important that the benefits of use are acknowledged, as well as the benefits of change, so that people can be fully aware of their attachment to the behavior. When they are ready to make a decision—when the decisional balance is tipped toward not using—they are entering the preparation stage.

**Preparation**

|  |  |
|---|---|
| *Tasks:* | Increase commitment. |
|  | Create a change plan. |
| *Goal:* | Have an action plan to be implemented in the near future. |
| *Processes of Change:* | Cognitive/experiential (internal) processes peak and begin to become less important. The behavioral (external) process of self-liberation (making choices and taking responsibility) is very important. Stimulus control and counterconditioning begin to assume importance in creating commitment and making the plan. |

Taking action does not automatically follow the decision to change. There are intermediary steps. A person must shore up her commitment to change and create an effective plan. Clients can use the information gleaned in the contemplation stage to good effect in creating their plans, which should fit their own personal needs. One size does not fit all in this endeavor. The client is the one who best understands his pattern and history of use, and it is the wisdom and knowledge of the client that is best used to develop the plan. Thus, you create a plan in collaboration with the client.

In this stage, the client is still engaging the internal processes of change, but a shift begins to the external processes. Self-liberation (making a choice and taking responsibility) becomes very important in this planning stage. As the client prepares for action, she also makes initial use of stimulus control (altering the triggers) and counterconditioning (altering responses to triggers).

As in the contemplation stage, the impulsivity and low

tolerance for delayed gratification that are characteristic of people who are addicted also present particular challenges for the clinician. People who are addicted are often reluctant to plan. Once again, the exploring and accepting posture of motivational interviewing is your ally.

## Strategies for Enhancing Commitment

*Making a Verbal Declaration*

While there has not been a lot of research on enhancing commitment, it is known that verbalizing commitments is an effective measure. A public declaration of intent suggests accountability, even if that public is only the clinician who is working with the client. Making an announcement that you are going to do something raises the stakes. If others know of your decision, it increases the expectation for action. It is useful to confirm with the person: "Have you made a firm decision that you want to change this addictive behavior?" or "Where are you in the process? What do you want to do now? Are you clear that you have decided to change your behavior?"

*Setting a Date*

Asking the person to set a date is also important. If the client declines to set a date, he has moved back into the contemplation stage. Suppose he says, "All right, I'll start sometime next week." You might respond, "That's good, but what would it take to get the day firmed up?" Research suggests that specificity promotes action.[5]

*Offering Choices*

Offering choices increases client investment and the effectiveness of the plan. There are a wide variety of programs and approaches available, including inpatient, outpatient, AA, and even initially, just cutting back. While cutting back is not the goal, it can be an important intermediary step toward the goal. By this time in the stages of change, people are beginning to cut down anyway. You can ask questions that will help clients think through which type of program, if any, they wish to attend. You can give them assignments to gather information about different programs, both by getting literature and by talking to people at different programs. You can also give information on adjunctive medications for their consideration.

*Increasing Self-Efficacy*
Increasing a person's confidence that she will be able to change a certain behavior is important in reinforcing commitment. It is also a marker of movement toward the action stage. The clinician can offer words of encouragement, help the client look at past successes, coach positive self-talk ("I can get through this dinner meeting without a glass of wine"), suggest affirmations ("I am courageous"), and help the client to imagine success ("I see myself looking happy and relaxed talking with friends and drinking tea").

This strategy, as well as the other strategies for enhancing commitment, are aimed at engaging the change process that TTM calls self-liberation (making a choice and taking responsibility).

**Strategies for Creating the Plan**
This brings us to creating the plan. The plan should be specific, workable for the individual, and comprehensive. More comprehensive planning seems to improve outcomes significantly. Specifically, data suggests that outcomes are better when more services are accessible to address the various needs of the individual trying to change an addictive behavior.[6]

An action plan will include both a change plan and a treatment plan. The change plan refers to the alterations a person makes in his personal, daily life outside of the treatment room. The treatment plan includes how the person will use treatment options to support the change plan. This involves making choices about inpatient versus outpatient treatment, how often to attend a treatment group, whether and when to go to family night, and so on.

What goes into the change plan? The following should be included: the specific change desired, the means to be used, the people who can help and how, what success will look like, and what could go wrong. Essentially clients look at what causes them to drink or use and then figure out what they need to support them in making the change. It can be helpful to write out a formal plan that clients can hold in their hands and look at. Exercise 3: Change Plan Worksheet (found on page 91 in appendix E) can help your clients focus on their plan. Make copies of the exercise and go over it with your clients.[7]

How do you go about making the plan? Using the following sections as a guide, explore with your clients both the situations they need to address and the skills they may need to acquire.

*Looking at a Person's Use Patterns and Past Attempts to Quit*
Understanding the client's habitual patterns of behavior is critical in this stage. Explore the situations, the times of day, and the environments in which the client typically uses. You can use the information gleaned in self-monitoring or from probing conversations with the client.

Does she take her first drink in what's been called the "arsenic hour"—the late afternoon when she and the kids are tired and hungry and she's cooking dinner? The change plan may require her to alter her environment at this time of day. Perhaps it would help if she made simpler dinners or did some of the preparation earlier in the day. Or does she binge on weekends when she is hanging out with friends who drink heavily? This may require planning different activities with different people on the weekends.

Learning to respond differently is another option and can include strategies such as desensitization, relaxation training, distraction, and constructive self-talk. These strategies are aimed at engaging the change processes that TTM identifies as stimulus control (altering or avoiding triggers) and counterconditioning (changing your response to a trigger).

*Identifying Needed Skills*
Planning also involves looking at problematic situations or feelings that overwhelm a person and that he uses alcohol or other drugs to cope. Did he relapse the last time he tried to quit after he didn't get a promotion he thought he should have gotten at work? When he was feeling overwhelming anger at his wife? When he was feeling overwhelmed by a sense of helplessness?

Addictive behaviors are often a coping mechanism, a way to deal with stressful feelings and situations. Developing coping skills gives the person an alternative to using alcohol or other drugs. If alcohol has been used to soothe anger, the person may need to develop anger management skills. The person may need to learn assertiveness skills to avoid becoming a victim again. Communication skills or negotiating skills may be needed to relieve tension on a job or in relationships.

*Identifying People Who Can Help*
The client may be able to identify people in her normal living environment who are supportive. Perhaps the client's family members do not use heavily or at all and are willing and able to provide support. Perhaps she has a number of friends in her circle who are rooting for her to change and will be available to encourage her and listen to her.

However, for those who lack helpful friends and family and for those who need additional assistance, more formal structures like AA can be invaluable in providing support. You can emphasize to a client the value of finding a sponsor. These people have wisdom acquired through hard experience and a commitment to be available whenever they are needed. There are also alternative Twelve Step facilitation groups, such as Women for Sobriety or Smart Recovery, that may fit a given person's needs or preferences.

*Addressing Other Complications*

The action plan may require that other problems be addressed if they are not to sabotage the change plan for stopping the addictive behavior. If not already addressed, dual diagnoses should typically begin to be addressed in this stage. A person who is chronically depressed may find it extremely difficult not to turn to alcohol or other drugs to soothe the pain. Antidepressant medication or therapy or both may be critical to following a plan. An anxiety disorder may require specific treatment as well. Chronic pain may require visits to a pain clinic to learn relaxation or other methods for coping with the pain.

Job loss and lack of housing can also generate stress and reduce options for handling difficult situations that trigger use. In these cases, a plan may include job training or other forms of education, making contact with social service agencies that can help with assistance, or developing skills to ask for help and to tolerate the frustration of bureaucracies.

■

A clinician's role in helping a client who is in the preparation stage is to bolster his commitment and help him develop a specific plan, one that is tailored to his personal needs and situation. The effectiveness of the plan can only be judged in the action stage.

## Action

| | |
|---|---|
| *Tasks:* | Implement strategies for change. |
| | Revise plan as needed. |
| | Sustain commitment in face of difficulties. |
| *Goal:* | Take successful action to change current behavior pattern and maintain pattern for three to six months. |
| *Processes of Change:* | Stimulus control, counterconditioning, and reinforcement management are needed to create change. Self-liberation sustains commitment. Helping relationships support change. |

Stepping into the action stage is qualitatively different than the steps taken in the earlier stages. Here, people break the physiological, psychological, and social ties that bind them to their addictive behavior. In the early part of this stage, people encounter a lot of pain and little sense of reward. It is especially important that they have a strong commitment to sustain them in the early part of the action stage and that they receive a great deal of support.

While there is no single right way to get through the early part of action, we do know that there is a common path people walk. Research demonstrates that it is at this point that people engage in the behavioral processes of change. They are making choices, avoiding triggers, responding in new ways, experiencing rewards for change, and developing supportive relationships. Strategically, then, the key is to help people engage in these behavioral processes. Part of this may be treatment, but that isn't always the case. And even when people do go to treatment, it is, of course, far from uniformly successful. It may be a first step, but it is less than half the battle. The key is to engage fully in the behavioral processes of change.

Sometimes beginning engagement in these processes is more easily done in residential treatment where people can get intense support to break the personal connections to the addictive behavior. Research suggests that people with greater alcohol involvement do better in more intensive treatment and have better psychosocial outcomes. Research has also indicated that three-year outcomes were better for outpatients who lived in alcohol-saturated environments if they were treated in the Twelve Step facilitation program and used the support of AA groups.[8]

### *Revising the Plan*

As someone implements her plan, she will find problems and roadblocks. It is critical to explore with her what is working and what is not, and then help her revise the plan. Perhaps she decided that she could go to a restaurant that serves wine for her weekly night-out dinner with her husband, but she is so conditioned to a good bottle of wine with any nice dinner in a restaurant that she finds this really painful. Or maybe it's impossible. Perhaps she ordered the bottle. Then the plan needs to be changed so that the weekly night out focuses on a different activity, at least until counterconditioning has successfully occurred, until the association between good food and good wine is no longer so intense.

### *Providing Support and Coaching*

Counterconditioning—learning new responses to old triggers—is both extremely difficult in the early part of the action stage and critical, especially as people move out of protected treatment environments and into the broad arenas of their lives. Here is where techniques such as acupuncture, meditation, hypnosis, and similar relaxation strategies can be helpful. You can also teach people urge surfing, in which they wait out the urge by pretending they are on a wave and riding the wave into the shore. They learn and begin to have confidence that the urge will pass.

***Devising and Recognizing Rewards***
Reinforcement of positive behaviors is critical, especially in the early part of the action stage. Addictive behaviors are so strong precisely because they have immediate and consistent reinforcement. People need reinforcement for alternative behaviors as well. You might suggest that a client count the money he saves when he no longer buys cigarettes, alcohol, or other drugs. AA tokens or chips for milestones can provide important rewards. Relationships can also provide important rewards in this stage. This can be the relationship with the clinician, who is recognizing and appreciating the client's efforts and successes. It can also be the relationship with a significant other, which may be more satisfying when the client has gained some sobriety.

    New reinforcement and rewards need to be added as the person moves further into the action stage. Alternative activities may provide rewards. Perhaps the person has begun a regular workout program after work to divert her attention at the time when she would have been drinking. As the workout program goes on, she will experience the rewards of feeling better, having more energy, and perhaps having her clothes fit better. One of your roles as a clinician can be to elicit the client's interests or suggest other activities, and then help the client recognize and articulate the rewards she is experiencing.

■

In the action stage, your role as a clinician is to hang in there, support your client, help him revise his plan, help him notice the rewards he is experiencing or develop new ones, refer him to appropriate resources, and stand by and give encouragement as he changes his behavior. After the client has sustained this new behavior for three to six months, he has tolerated the initial breaking of the ties to the addictive behavior and established a new pattern. At this point he enters maintenance.

### Maintenance

|  |  |
|---|---|
| *Tasks:* | Sustain change over time and across a wide variety of situations. |
| *Goal:* | Maintain long-term change of the old pattern and continued practice of a new pattern of behavior. |
| *Processes of Change:* | The behavioral processes of reinforcement management and counterconditioning provide competing rewards. Helping relationships support abstinence. Experiential processes of consciousness raising and self-reevaluation protect against problematic thinking patterns. |

In the action stage, the client stopped the addictive behavior. To sustain recovery, new behaviors and rewards must be integrated; they must become part of the way she lives her life. This stage is marked by significantly increased confidence, fewer feelings of temptation, and the creation of a new life. The behavioral change processes continue to be primary, but consciousness raising and self-reevaluation may assume importance again as people cope with various feelings and awareness that are no longer masked by the addiction. The challenge in this stage is to cope with the infrequent trigger, which may catch the person unaware. Overconfidence and carelessness may also threaten maintenance, as can an erosion of commitment.

***Doing Checkups***

People generally are no longer in treatment or aftercare programs by the time they have reached the maintenance stage. However, this does not mean that they don't need support anymore. Follow-up is important. Clients should know they are always welcome to come in with concerns. But it's also valuable to schedule checkups, similar to dental hygiene checkups, perhaps every couple of months. During these sessions you can continue to offer reinforcement, help with problem solving, and examine any threats to sobriety.

***Addressing Multiple Problems***

The maintenance stage is an important time to fully examine the context of life issues and make sure they are being addressed. Significant unresolved issues can provoke relapse. This is an important time to work in-depth on marital problems, childhood abuse issues, depression, anxiety, social skills, or other family and environmental problems that cause too much stress.

This is also a time to simply support personal growth. You will want to focus on helping people create healthy sources of reinforcement, satisfaction, and meaning. As people are in the later phases of the action stage and continue on to maintenance, both the challenges and rewards of stopping the addictive behavior become more apparent and delineated. It may become apparent that your client's life feels empty without the addictive behavior, a condition that probably existed before the inception of the behavior, and he wants to work more actively on cultivating a spiritual component. This is an important time to work on the later AA steps, to look at opportunities missed and regrets for past actions, to deal with them, and to move on.

## Making Referrals

Appropriate referrals can be critical in this stage. It is very important to attain some level of stability in the context of life to support stabilization of sobriety. This may mean more work on job skills or returning to school. It may mean continued attendance of AA or other Twelve Step support groups. Or it may mean seeking more intensive individual or group therapy. As a clinician, you will also need to follow up on the referrals you have made, asking the client whether they were useful.

■

Maintenance goes beyond changing a specific addictive behavior to encompass the broad outlines of a person's life. To sustain recovery, a person must become healthy and grounded. She must create a life that is rewarding and seek significance and meaning in constructive and healthy ways. Ultimately, since recovery and sobriety become an integral part of a new life, the best protection against relapse is personal growth and self-development.

### Summary

All people go through predictable stages when they are making changes in their behavior, whether it's addictive behaviors or other unhealthy behaviors. The stages that have been identified are precontemplation, contemplation, preparation, action, and maintenance. Each stage requires unique tasks and has unique goals.

In precontemplation, a client must become aware that a problem exists in order to move on to the next stage. The contemplation stage requires a thorough and deep exploration of the costs and benefits of both continuing the addictive behavior and of changing. In the preparation stage, the client's commitment must be bolstered, and he must develop a plan tailored to his personal needs and situation. The action stage requires sustaining the commitment in the face of difficulties and revising the plan as needed. Finally, the maintenance stage involves a client integrating the behavior changes into her overall life and establishing a new pattern of behavior.

Bear in mind that an empathic approach—one that is accepting, empowering, and supportive of the client—is critical to engendering client motivation. Your values are not the important ones here. It's critical to elicit the client's real feelings and beliefs about his behavior. Movement to the next stage depends on the client's motivation to change and should not just be an attempt to avoid negative consequences or to please somebody else.

There are a wide variety of techniques that you can make use of to help clients change addictive and other undesirable behaviors, and the transtheoretical model of change provides an essential framework. Identifying what stage of change your clients are in can help you develop an appropriate and effective treatment plan for them.

➤

## Appendix A

# Alcohol (and Illegal Drugs) Decisional Balance Scale

Client ID#: _____

Date: _____ / _____ / _____

Assessment Point: _____

The following statements may play a part in making a decision about using alcohol (or other drugs). We would like to know how important each statement is to you at the present time in relation to making a decision. Rate each statement using the following five-point ranking system:

1 = Not important at all
2 = Slightly important
3 = Moderately important
4 = Very important
5 = Extremely important

Please read each statement and circle the number on the *right* to indicate how you rate its level of importance as it relates to your making a decision about whether to drink (or use drugs) at the present time.

Appendix A

| HOW IMPORTANT IS THIS TO ME? | IMPORTANCE IN MAKING A DECISION ABOUT DRINKING (DRUG USE): | | | | |
|---|---|---|---|---|---|
| | NOT AT ALL | SLIGHTLY | MODERATELY | VERY | EXTREMELY |
| 1. My drinking (drug use) causes problems with others. | 1 | 2 | 3 | 4 | 5 |
| 2. I like myself better when I am drinking (using drugs). | 1 | 2 | 3 | 4 | 5 |
| 3. Because I continue to drink (use drugs), some people think I lack the character to quit. | 1 | 2 | 3 | 4 | 5 |
| 4. Drinking (drug use) helps me deal with problems. | 1 | 2 | 3 | 4 | 5 |
| 5. Having to lie to others about my drinking (drug use) bothers me. | 1 | 2 | 3 | 4 | 5 |
| 6. Some people try to avoid me when I drink (use drugs). | 1 | 2 | 3 | 4 | 5 |
| 7. Drinking (drug use) helps me to have fun and socialize. | 1 | 2 | 3 | 4 | 5 |
| 8. Drinking (drug use) interferes with my functioning at home and/or at work. | 1 | 2 | 3 | 4 | 5 |
| 9. Drinking (drug use) makes me more of a fun person. | 1 | 2 | 3 | 4 | 5 |
| 10. Some people close to me are disappointed in me because of my drinking (drug use). | 1 | 2 | 3 | 4 | 5 |
| 11. Drinking (drug use) helps me to loosen up and express myself. | 1 | 2 | 3 | 4 | 5 |
| 12. I seem to get myself into trouble when drinking (using drugs). | 1 | 2 | 3 | 4 | 5 |

Duplicating this page for personal or group use is permissible.

*Alcohol (and Illegal Drugs) Decisional Balance Scale*

| HOW IMPORTANT IS THIS TO ME? | IMPORTANCE IN MAKING A DECISION ABOUT DRINKING (DRUG USE): | | | | |
|---|---|---|---|---|---|
| | NOT AT ALL | SLIGHTLY | MODERATELY | VERY | EXTREMELY |
| 13. I could accidentally hurt someone because of my drinking (drug use). | 1 | 2 | 3 | 4 | 5 |
| 14. Not drinking (using drugs) at a social gathering would make me feel too different. | 1 | 2 | 3 | 4 | 5 |
| 15. I am losing the trust and respect of my co-workers and/or spouse because of my drinking (drug use). | 1 | 2 | 3 | 4 | 5 |
| 16. My drinking (drug use) helps give me energy and keeps me going. | 1 | 2 | 3 | 4 | 5 |
| 17. I am more sure of myself when I am drinking (using drugs). | 1 | 2 | 3 | 4 | 5 |
| 18. I am setting a bad example for others with my drinking (drug use). | 1 | 2 | 3 | 4 | 5 |
| 19. Without alcohol (illegal drugs), my life would be dull and boring. | 1 | 2 | 3 | 4 | 5 |
| 20. People seem to like me better when I am drinking (using drugs). | 1 | 2 | 3 | 4 | 5 |

**Scoring:**

Pros of drinking (drug use) are items 2, 4, 7, 9, 11, 14, 16, 17, 19, 20.

Cons of drinking (drug use) are items 1, 3, 5, 6, 8, 10, 12, 13, 15, 18.

To get the average number of pros endorsed, add up the total number of points from the "pro" items and divide by 10. Example: Pros of drinking (drug use) = Sum of items (2+4+7+9+11+14+16+17+19+20) divided by 10.

To get the average number of cons endorsed, add up the total number of points from the "con" items and divide by 10. Example: Cons of drinking (drug use) = Sum of i (1+3+5+6+8+10+12+13+15+18) divided by 10.

Appendix A

The preceding worksheet is taken from appendix B of *Enhancing Motivation for Change in Substance Abuse Treatment*, Treatment Improvement Protocol (TIP) Series, No. 35.[1] It can be duplicated without permission. It can also be ordered from the SAMHSA Web site at

www.treatment.org/Externals/tips.html

Or it can be downloaded at

www.ncbi.nlm.nih.gov/books/bv.fcgi?rid=hstat5.chapter.61302

## Appendix B

# Brief Situational Confidence Questionnaire (BSCQ)

The Brief Situational Confidence Questionnaire (BSCQ) can be found in appendix B of *Enhancing Motivation for Change in Substance Abuse Treatment,* Treatment Improvement Protocol (TIP) Series, No. 35[1] or by writing to its author:

Linda Sobell, Ph.D.
Nova Southeastern University
Center for Psychological Studies
3301 College Avenue
Fort Lauderdale, FL 33314
Phone: (954) 262-5811
Fax: (954) 262-3857
E-mail: sobelll@nsu.nova.edu

A sample electronic version of the BSCQ can be found at

www.ncbi.nlm.nih.gov/books/bv.fcgi?rid=hstat5.chapter.61302

## Appendix C

# Alcohol Abstinence Self-Efficacy Scale (AASE)[1]

The AASE assesses Albert Bandura's construct of self-efficacy and evaluates an individual's efficacy (i.e., confidence) to abstain from drinking in twenty situations that represent typical drinking cues. These situations form four subscales, comprising five items each, which examine cues related to negative affect, social/positive situations, physical and other concerns, and withdrawal and urges. In addition, these same items can be assessed to evaluate an individual's temptation to drink, providing a measure of cue strength to relate to the efficacy evaluation. Both efficacy and temptation are rated on five-point Likert scales ranging from "not at all" to "extremely." Individuals are asked to give a current estimate of temptation and efficacy. These scales can be used to evaluate individuals entering treatment, progress during treatment, relapse potential, and posttreatment functioning.

### Target Population

Adults

The AASE would be especially helpful to personnel in treatment programs where the goal of intervention is abstinence. It could also be used to evaluate AA program participation or for outcome evaluations and program evaluation. The AASE could be used for adolescents if the goal for these individuals is abstinence from alcohol.

Appendix C

## Administrative Issues

- Twenty efficacy and twenty temptation items, four subscales
- Pencil and paper self-administered
- Time required: ten minutes
- No training required for administration

## Scoring

- Time required: five to ten minutes
- Scored by hand
- No computerized scoring or interpretation available
- Normed on outpatient substance abusers

## Psychometrics

Reliability studies done:
    Internal consistency

Measures of validity derived:
    Construct

## Clinical Utility of Instrument

The AASE yields clients' evaluations of their perceived temptation to drink and their efficacy to abstain in twenty common situations. Individuals who score high in temptation and low in efficacy across all situations are more dependent. Individuals who respond differently to specific situations could be given more specific interventions. Clinicians could also give the measure repeatedly to assess progress in treatment in terms of these self-evaluations. Finally, relapse prevention programs could use these estimates of temptation and efficacy to individualize and guide treatment.

## Research Applicability

Self-efficacy can be used as either an outcome measure or a mediator of drinking outcomes. This scale is comparable to ones used for nicotine dependence, eating disorders, and substance abuse, so self-efficacy could be comparatively evaluated across behaviors. The measure can also be used to track progress during treatment. Scores can be used in latent growth analyses, as well as in more traditional multiwave analyses. Efficacy scores have been found to vary with stage of change and to be responsive to relapse threats, so they could be used in relapse studies.

## Copyright, Cost, and Source Issues

This instrument is in the public domain and may be obtained free of charge by contacting its author:

> Carlo C. DiClemente, Ph.D.
> Professor and Chair
> University of Maryland, Baltimore County
> Department of Psychology
> 1000 Hilltop Circle
> Baltimore, MD 21250
> Phone: (410) 455-2415
> Fax: (410) 455-1055
> E-mail: diclemen@umbc.edu
> www.umbc.edu/psyc/habits

A PDF file of the AASE is also available at

> adai.washington.edu/instruments/pdf/AASE.pdf

or at

> www.umbc.edu/psyc/habits

## Source Reference

DiClemente, C. C., J. P. Carbonari, R. P. G. Montgomery, and S. O. Hughes. "The Alcohol Abstinence Self-Efficacy Scale." *J Stud Alcohol* 55 (1994): 141–48.

## Supporting References

Ito, J. R., D. M. Donovan, and J. J. Hall. "Relapse Prevention in Alcohol Aftercare: Effects on Drinking Outcome, Change Process, and Aftercare Attendance." *Br J Addict* 83 (1988): 171–81.

Project MATCH Research Group. "Project MATCH: Rationale and Methods for a Multisite Clinical Trial Matching Alcoholism Patients to Treatment." *Alcoholism Clin Exp Res* 17 (1993): 1130–45.

DiClemente, C. C., S. F. Fairhurst, and N. Piotrowski. "Efficacy in the Addictive Behaviors." In *Self-Efficacy, Adaptation, and Adjustment: Theory, Research, and Application*. Edited by J. E. Maddux. New York: Plenum Press, in press.

# Appendix D

# The University of Rhode Island Change Assessment Scale (URICA)[1]

This thirty-two–item scale assesses attitudes toward changing problem behaviors (using the stages of change construct from the transtheoretical model). Eight items assess each of four stages: precontemplation, contemplation, action, and maintenance. Subjects are asked to endorse these statements using a Likert scale of 1 (not at all) to 5 (extremely) in response to how important each statement is to them. Items are summed to give a total score for each stage.

### Target Population
Both inpatient and outpatient adults

### Administrative Issues
- Thirty-two items
- Pencil and paper self-administered
- Time required: five to ten minutes
- Requires low to moderate reading level

### Scoring
Norms available for outpatient alcoholism treatment population
Can be used with computer-scannable forms

## Psychometrics

Reliability studies done:
    Internal consistency

Measures of validity derived:
    Construct

## Clinical Utility of Instrument

Assessment of stages of change/readiness construct can be used as a predictor of behavioral change, for treatment matching, and also as outcome variables.

## Research Applicability

May be used in research with clinical populations for both outcome and process research.

## Copyright, Cost, and Source Issues

This instrument is in the public domain and may be obtained free of charge by contacting its author:

   Carlo C. DiClemente, Ph.D.
   Professor and Chair
   University of Maryland, Baltimore County
   Department of Psychology
   1000 Hilltop Circle
   Baltimore, MD 21250
   Phone: (410) 455-2415
   Fax: (410) 455-1055
   E-mail: diclemen@umbc.edu
   www.umbc.edu/psyc/habits

A copy of the form can also be found at

   www.umbc.edu/psyc/habits/URICA%20psychotherapy.htm

   or

   www.uri.edu/research/cprc/Measures/urica.htm

## Source Reference

McConnaughy, E. A., J. O. Prochaska, and W. F. Velicer. "Stages of Change in Psychotherapy: Measurement and Sample Profiles." *Psychotherapy: Theory, Research, and Practice* 20 (1983): 368–75.

## Supporting References

Willoughby, F. W., and J. F. Edens. "Construct Validity and Predictive Utility of the Stages of Change Scale for Alcoholics." *Journal of Substance Abuse* 8, no. 3 (1996): 275–91.

Carney, M. M., and D. R. Kivlahan. "Motivational Subtypes among Veterans Seeking Substance Abuse Treatment: Profiles Based on Stages of Change." *Psychology of Addictive Behaviors* 9, no. 2 (1995): 135–42.

DiClemente, C. C., and S. O. Hughes. "Stages of Change Profiles in Outpatient Alcoholism Treatment." *Journal of Substance Abuse* 2 (1990): 217–35.

## Appendix E

# Exercises

Exercise 1:
Readiness Ruler, 87

Exercise 2:
Decisional Balance Worksheet, 89

Exercise 3:
Change Plan Worksheet, 91

EXERCISE 1

# Readiness Ruler

Name _____

Date _____

```
| |  |  |  |  |  |  |  |  |  ||
 1   2   3   4   5   6   7   8   9   10
Not Ready        Unsure              Ready
```

EXERCISE 2

# Decisional Balance Worksheet

Name _____

Date _____

| **Continuing Behavior** | **Stopping Behavior** |
|---|---|
| Pros | Cons |
| | |
| | |
| | |
| | |
| Cons | Pros |
| | |
| | |
| | |
| | |

EXERCISE 3

# Change Plan Worksheet

Name _____

Date _____

---

The changes I want to make are:

_____

_____


The most important reasons I want to make these changes are:

_____

_____


My main goals for myself in making these changes are:

_____

_____


I plan to do these things to reach my goals:

| Plan of Action | When |
|---|---|
| | |
| | |
| | |
| | |
| | |

Exercise 3

The first steps I plan to take in changing are:

_____

_____

_____

Some things that could interfere with my plan are:

_____

_____

Other people could help me in changing in these ways:

    *Person*                          *Possible Ways to Help*

_____

_____

_____

_____

I hope that my plan will have these positive results:

_____

_____

_____

I will know that my plan is working if:

_____

_____

_____

# Notes

### Chapter 1: The Transtheoretical Model: What Is It?

1. M. Velasquez et al., *Group Treatment for Substance Abuse: A Stages-of-Change Therapy Manual* (New York: Guilford Press, 2001).
2. C. DiClemente, *Addiction and Change: How Addictions Develop and Addicted People Recover* (New York: Guilford Press, 2003).
3. Ibid., 36.
4. Ibid., 41.
5. Substance Abuse and Mental Health Services Administration (SAMHSA), Center for Substance Abuse Treatment (CSAT), *Enhancing Motivation for Change in Substance Abuse Treatment*, Treatment Improvement Protocol (TIP) Series, No. 35. (Rockville, Md.: U.S. Department of Health and Human Services, 1999), 19.
6. Ibid.

### Chapter 2: The Movement into Addiction

1. DiClemente, *Addiction and Change*, 68.
2. Ibid., 78.
3. Ibid., 78.
4. Ibid., 86.
5. Ibid., 46.
6. Ibid., 96.
7. Ibid., 104.
8. Ibid., 56.

### Chapter 3: Making an Assessment

1. DiClemente, *Addiction and Change*, 116–20.
2. Adapted from K. M. Tomlin and H. Richardson, *Motivational Interviewing and Stages of Change* (Center City, Minn.: Hazelden, 2004), 43.
3. SAMHSA, TIP No. 35, 43.
4. Ibid., 153–4.
5. P. A. Hays, *Addressing Cultural Complexities in Practice: A Framework for Clinicians and Counselors* (Washington, D.C.: American Psychological Association, 2001). D. W. Sue and D. Sue. *Counseling the Culturally Diverse: Theory and Practice*, 4th ed. (New

York: Wiley, 2002). SAMHSA, TIP No. 35 has general references. There is also a TIP on cultural competence currently being revised.

6. SAMHSA, TIP No. 35, 139.
7. Ibid., 63.
8. Ibid., 136–7.
9. Ibid., 137.
10. Substance Abuse and Mental Health Services Administration (SAMHSA), Center for Substance Abuse Treatment (CSAT), *Assessment and Treatment of Patients with Coexisting Mental Illness and Alcohol and Other Drug Use*, Treatment Improvement Protocol (TIP) Series, No. 9 (Rockville, Md.: U.S. Department of Health and Human Services, 1994). More information on this article can be found at www.treatment.org/Externals/tips.html or
www.ncbi.nlm.nih.gov/books/bv.fcgi?rid=hstat5.chapter.29713.

## Chapter 4: Practical Strategies for Helping People in Recovery

1. DiClemente, *Addiction and Change*, 123.
2. W. R. Miller and S. Rollnick, *Motivational Interviewing: Preparing People to Change Addictive Behavior* (New York: Guilford Press, 1991).
3. W. R. Miller and S. Rollnick, *Motivational Interviewing: Preparing People for Change*, 2d. ed. (New York: Guilford Press, 2002); Tomlin and Richardson, *Motivational Interviewing and Stages of Change*.
4. SAMHSA, TIP No. 35, 72.
5. DiClemente, *Addiction and Change*, 111.
6. Ibid., 113.
7. Ibid., 159.
8. Ibid., 180–1.

## Appendix A:
## Alcohol (and Illegal Drugs) Decisional Balance Scale

1. SAMHSA, TIP No. 35, 189–91.

## Appendix B:
## Brief Situational Confidence Questionnaire (BSCQ)

1. SAMHSA, TIP No. 35, 204–5.

**Appendix C:**
**Alcohol Abstinence Self-Efficacy Scale (AASE)**

1. The information in appendix C was reproduced from the following Web site: www.umbc.edu/psyc/habits.

**Appendix D:**
**The University of Rhode Island Change Assessment Scale (URICA)**

1. The information in appendix D was reproduced from the following Web sites: www.niaaa.nih.gov/publications/urica.htm and www.umbc.edu/psyc/habits.

## About the Author

**Carlo C. DiClemente, Ph.D.,** is professor and chair for the Department of Psychology, University of Maryland, Baltimore County. He is internationally recognized as cocreator (with James Prochaska, Ph.D.) of the transtheoretical model of change, more commonly referred to as the stages of change. He is the author or coauthor of more than 140 publications, including a popular book on the stages, *Changing for Good* (Avon 1995). DiClemente has received the American Psychological Association's Distinguished Contribution Award from Division 50, was named Researcher of the Year by the Maryland Psychological Association in 1992, and was selected to receive the Robert Wood Johnson Foundation's Innovators Combating Substance Abuse award. His latest book, *Addiction and Change: How Addictions Develop and Addicted People Recover*, was published by Guilford Press.

**Hazelden Publishing and Educational Services** is a division of the Hazelden Foundation, a not-for-profit organization. Since 1949, Hazelden has been a leader in promoting the dignity and treatment of people afflicted with the disease of chemical dependency.

The mission of the foundation is to improve the quality of life for individuals, families, and communities by providing a national continuum of information, education, and recovery services that are widely accessible; to advance the field through research and training; and to improve our quality and effectiveness through continuous improvement and innovation.

Stemming from that, the mission of this division is to provide quality information and support to people wherever they may be in their personal journey—from education and early intervention, through treatment and recovery, to personal and spiritual growth.

Although our treatment programs do not necessarily use everything Hazelden publishes, our bibliotherapeutic materials support our mission and the Twelve Step philosophy upon which it is based. We encourage your comments and feedback.

The headquarters of the Hazelden Foundation are in Center City, Minnesota. Additional treatment facilities are located in Chicago, Illinois; Newberg, Oregon; New York, New York; Plymouth, Minnesota; St. Paul, Minnesota; and West Palm Beach, Florida. At these sites, we provide a continuum of care for men and women of all ages. Our Plymouth facility is designed specifically for youth and families.

For more information on Hazelden, please call **1-800-257-7800**.

Or you may access our World Wide Web site on the Internet at **www.hazelden.org**.